Kathi;

God blessings Always

Love

[illegible]

5-15-2022

Speaking to Heaven

Our Loved Ones are only a Breath Away

Joseph LoBrutto III

Our Never Ending Journey of Life Series

United States of America 2016

Speaking to Heaven

Our Loved Ones are Only a Breath Away

Copyright © 2016 by Joseph LoBrutto III
www.OurJourneyOfLife.com

Table of Contents

Foreword

By Howard Carter III

I recently spent time with the Rev. Joseph LoBrutto as he shared his gift of being a direct link to Heaven, delivering compassionate messages to heal the soul and teaching us how it all began. The force has always been strong with Joseph, the "Man of God", even when he was just a child of God. He reflects back to his earliest memories of collecting figures of Saints like most kids would collect baseball cards. Every Sunday at his church he would use his allowance to buy Saints and place them on his windowsill. This was not an ordinary hobby, but then again this was not an ordinary boy. Ordinary boys don't see dead people. Later in life, Joseph would become a channel, then a medium and eventually a healer for those in need, thereby making him a saint of sorts to those he has helped.

He has had special abilities all of his life. In childhood, spirits used to visit him but he thought they were regular people. He didn't know the difference until his grandmother passed away when he was ten years old. He attended her funeral and then a few days later when he entered his bedroom he found her sitting on his bed smiling at him. That is how he realized that he could see spirits. After that he recalls being so frightened that he slept underneath the covers with the lights on so he would stop seeing spirits. He now realized that the parade of people coming in and out of his room were spirits and he wanted them to go away, which they eventually did. The nightmare of every kid that the boogieman is under the bed was true for little Joseph, but with his continued resistance it eventually went away and did not return until he was in his twenties.

Around that time he began channeling spirit guides, but it wasn't until his cousin Joey passed away suddenly at the age of 34 that Joseph finally began to take his gift seriously.

Joseph recalls that after Joey's funeral he was driving home and heard Joey's voice. When he looked over he saw his deceased cousin sitting there on the passenger seat passionately begging Joseph to go talk to his wife. Because he had died very suddenly of a heart attack, his cousin just wanted to say his final goodbye to the love of his life.

Years later, now fully active in his psychic medium practice, Joseph visited Brazil and met with John of God. John of God is a highly renowned Mediumistic healer. Five thousand people a week visit Brazil for healing from John of God. It was this great man that foretold of Joseph's healing gifts and inspired Joseph to move towards his destiny as a healer. Today many people have experienced miraculous healing from major diseases and from physical and emotional traumas, as well as receiving spiritual balance for a healthy mind, body and soul through Joseph. All of this healing comes from God working through Joseph in his Divine Energy Healing.

I asked Joseph what channeling feels like and he said, "It's a conscious thought that moves in; it's almost like putting on a raincoat. You don't check out of your body, and the spirit guide does not check in, but we merge." He further reflects on where the title 'Man of God' came into play. "I was tapping into The Christ Consciousness of The Masters Jesus and Joshua and bringing their spiritual information through; that led me to writing books and recording audiobooks."

To date Joseph has produced a book which is now published in a variety of languages called "Is There More to Life Than What We Know?", an audiobook recording "The Promise", a deck of Universal Energy and Divine Affirmations cards, Divine Affirmation CDs, and a "Speaking to Heaven Meditation" CD. He continually appears in "Speaking to Heaven" and "Divine Healing" galleries around the world. For those who are open to his healing energy, he has much to offer. This is the story of Joseph's continuing journey of life as he connects us with the heavenly energy of God.

Acknowledgments

I would like to thank God for the gifts that have been bestowed on me as well as the wisdom of my Spirit Guides of the Collective; they have been a wonderful influence on my life. I also would like to thank my parents, Joe and Carmen, and my children for their love and support of my work. I would like to give a special thank you to Betânia Valante for her inspiration in helping me stay focused in the work that I do and for giving me the idea to write this book. I am also grateful to my staff members Staci Lord, Nicole Paulino, and Teri Miller – it's because of you that I am successful. I would also like to thank Mary Collins for her hard work and journalistic attentions in helping me to create an informative book of heaven.

It's been an incredible journey so far and I want to thank you and everyone who has supported my work as a medium. I also would like to thank all of the crossed-over loved ones with whom I have connected in the past and with whom I will connect in the future for choosing me as the medium to deliver their messages to you. Life is a journey and we are here to make the best of it, so whatever life may bring, look at it as an adventure and a learning experience. If you look at life this way you will find that life is not as hard as it seems and you will be closer to heaven than you think!

Tribute to my Father

February 19th 1933- April 1, 2019

For the past few days my family and I have been preparing for my father Joseph LoBrutto Jr. to make his journey into heaven. He has been admitted to hospice care at the Veterans Hospital in West Palm Beach Florida. Served in Korea and is a decorated Marine " Semper Fidelis. "

I'm here this morning with my mother who herself is ill with stage 5 dementia. In this stage she has a hard time understanding and keeps asking me is my father going to get better. The hospice priest made a visit as well and offered a prayer of healing and communion to my mother and myself.

During his prayer he forgave my father for all of his sins and I had to think does my father have any sins? I have known him as a remarkable humble man who wouldn't hurt anyone. He always supported me in life and was always there for my brother and I when we needed him. He is a loving husband , father and grandfather.

I have always felt that God has given me the strength to do the work of a medium to help people who are in my situation but now that it's close to home I find myself grief stricken. I know that there is a heaven because I feel it every time I connect with a passed over loved one. I only wish I could share this with my father who is not aware of his surroundings or his family by his side. I whisper in his ear every day more then once that it is ok to let go. But I watch him holding on to every breath and at times calling out loud for his Ma Ma and Papa just stubborn not to let go.

As I sit here by myself with him I began to see my grandparents and all of his siblings standing by his bed as I wonder if he is aware that they are here in the room. I ask them to please help my father to cross over peacefully. Then they will show me that they will have a big welcome home party for him, Italian style! I see that the table is set with grandmas cooking for his welcome home to reunite with his parents and siblings. It will be a wonderful surprise for him that I know. So for the days to come it's a waiting game to see when he is ready to make the transition. All I can do is pray for his peaceful transition into heaven. I love you dad and will look for you on the other side.

The Eulogy

We are gathered here today to say good bye to my father Joe LoBrutto. It is difficult, at best to stand before you and to attempt to honor my father with words. It's never an easy task to capture someone in a speech as words will sometime fall short in capturing someones true essence.

My mother carmen would always say to people how he was a wonderful and caring husband and that their love was an example of how a marriage should be. My brother Robert would tell me how much he admires our dad because he was always there for him and reassures him about how much he loves him. I want to thank my brother Robert for being the caretaker of my dad while he suffered through Parkinson. I believed my dad lived a longer life because of the home care that was provided for him through our family.

Growing up my dad was a warm caring father to Robert and I. He would read us bedtime stories and when we were sick he would be the one to rub vics on our chest and tuck us in bed.

He was also known as Mr. Fix It! Always tinkering around in his garage and between my brother and I he restored my 66 Mustang, my brothers Jeep and many other cars we went through. I can remember him rolling his eyes when I asked him for a drumset and the very next day he was sound proofing my bedroom lol.

My dad loved his family and became an instant grandfather early in his life. He loved his grandchildren and always got excited when they visited. He owned the first generation of video cameras and his grandkids became his center of attention. Watching family videos he would talk into the camera showing that the fishing poles and boat were ready for the kids. When he would visit our home on Christmas day he would have a big smile on his faces singing Christmas jingles for his grandkids bearing gifts from a large laundry bag.

My mother would share with me when they first met. My father was a photographer and my mother worked at the Kodak factory proofing photos. My mother was just fresh off the boat from Puerto Rico and didn't speak english. So he jester to her to remove her gloves off her hands. You are properly wondering why he did this? He wanted to see if she had a wedding ring on her finger. Needless to say they fell in loved and been together for over sixty years.

Both Robert and I followed dads foot steps in careers. For those who know me I have been a professional photographer / videographer just like my dad and my brother Robert was been partners with my father in the Dry-cleaning business for over forty years.

Having just boys my dad had to learn to adjust to how to handle girls when his granddaughters Ashley and Jessica came along. What grandpa loved about Ashley was how her expressions where very theatrical. She would get excited about the little things. I have a video showing when she was excited about her grandpa baiting her fish hook only to begin to feel sorry for the poor worm. My dad always enjoy the plays that Ashley would coordinate with her siblings. There are many skits showing all of them dancing and singing.

Jessica was the one who spent most of her toddler and preschool years with my parents. He was so patient with her while he would sit in his recliner as Jessica would experiment with halloween makeup on her grandpa. Their home would become the party house for Jessica and her friends because of the pool. I just learned yesterday that while my parents were on a cruise Jessica secretly had a college pool party with friends at their home. It was my parents who made it possible for Jessica to attend college and I remember my father telling me that she was the only one in our family to graduate college and I'm so proud of our little girl.

Boys will be boys and when my dad thought he was done with Robert and I, then came his grandsons Todd and Adam into his life. Todd was always laid back and just loved visiting his grandparents as a child. Sports was Todd's thing and he would always talk about the Miami dolphins with his grandpa. Adam was always under grandpas feet and loved to tinker with things just as much as his grandpa. They had a special bond between them, my father will tell me how proud he was of Adam for serving our country.

Both my father and Adam served in Japan Headquarters 3rd Battalion 12th Marines. My father served in Korea and is a decorated marine. During the last days in hospice Adam made every effort to be there with his grandfather. Adam works for the Veterans Affairs and I thank him for helping to arrange for his grandfathers care at the Veterans hospital and military burial.

I had a wonderful gift given to me last month when I was the sole care taker for my dad for a couple of weeks. It wasn't easy and I give praise to my brother Robert for the outstanding job he did. But I would give anything to have the responsibly in taking care of him once again. My father made me for who I am today and I thank God that I had a father in my life who inspired me to achieve all my accomplishments. He was there when I came into this world and I was there when he left. I wanted to be there with him when he passed so I can keep reassuring him about how much everyone loved him and Robert and I will take care of mom. As a child I can remember the big family Italian gathering at my grandparents house and I kepted telling my dad as he was dying that everyone is there in heaven celebrating your welcome home.

God bless you dad, I love you and we all will miss you.
~Joey

Introduction

It's been a few years since I wrote my first book *"Is There More to Life Than What We Know?"*. In my early writings, I was at the beginning of my journey of learning to adapt to my gifts and obtaining the courage to share them with the world. It all began with the movie "Out on a Limb" where I saw Shirley MacClaine meeting with a channel. This is what inspired me to learn channeling myself as I began to communicate with my spirit guides that I call "The Collective". You can learn about "The Collective" in my first book. I always tell people that God granted me the gift to communicate with loved ones who have crossed over and it has given me great pleasure to help in the healing process for those who have lost someone.

As a professional medium, my job is to show evidence that our loved ones are still a part of our lives even though they are no longer here. People often ask me how I make contact with spirits. They want to know if the spirit shows its presence to me like the television show "Ghost Whisperer" or in the movie "The Sixth Sense". I tell them that it's more like being an interpreter who speaks and thinks in two languages at once. I am able to bridge the gap between two planes of existence - that of the living and that of the spirit world - by being clairsentient, which simply means 'clear feeling' or the ability to feel the emotions and personalities of the deceased. The deceased will plant a thought, an image, or a name into my mind and I will acquire the message from there. After I receive validation that I'm connecting with the deceased person, the information will come through in a straightforward manner.

I am also known as a “direct dial”, meaning that by knowing the relationship of the spirit with whom you seek to communicate, my accuracy rate is 95% for being able to connect with them. I tell people it’s like having a universal phone book! After the loss of a dear friend or loved one, we sometimes wish we could speak with them. While on the earth plane, we sense that the spiritual realm, heaven, is a beautiful and wonderful place. People with near death experiences usually want to stay. Oftentimes our loved ones will send us a sign to comfort us shortly after they depart, such as a scent of flowers, tobacco, or perfume, or they will create the sensation of a soft touch on the arm or shoulder. Sometimes we may just sense their presence or we may dream and have visions of our loved ones. They don’t want to scare us; they just want us to know that they are fine and still connected to us.

People often ask when is the best time to try to connect with our loved ones. Upon losing a loved one, the first thing some people want to do is find a medium so they can contact the deceased. I suggest that people should wait a few weeks before doing so. As a medium my best advice is that when a person passes, it’s best to give them some time before trying to contact them. They, too, are grieving and adjusting to their death so the spirit also needs time to settle into their new state of consciousness. During the transition from being a physical being into a spirit being, an angel, spirit guide, friend or family member will be with them to help them with their grieving and their transition into heaven when they are ready to move on.
Our loved ones will attend their own funeral and check on us day and night after just passing. After a number of weeks, however, the energy of the spirit begins to weaken and the memory of the spirit’s life on earth begins to fade. They will have a strong desire to go into the light and their angels, guides, or a passed-over loved ones will help direct them.

When passing through the veil, the spirit is rejuvenated with God's energy, making it free of all earthly limitations. The spirit is united with its loved ones who have passed over previously, creating a whole new world for them to explore. It is time for them to begin their life in heaven as spirit. The memory of the spirit is restored and it will remember the life it once had and all of its memories. Remember that when it is time for you to cross over, your loved ones will be waiting for you to share their lives with you in heaven.

Heaven is also called the Astral Plane; it's the place of learning. Most people believe that heaven is beyond the stars and the universe. It is not. Heaven is within you; it's a breath away. When we whisper, our loved ones can hear us. There is no time in Heaven; what may have happened many years ago may seem to be only minutes in the astral realm. So if you lost a loved one many years ago, know that when it is your time to cross over, to them it will seem only minutes since they saw you last. Heaven is wherever or whatever you want it to be. If you feel that waterfalls, sunsets, sunrises and angels represent heaven to you, then that's the heaven you will have created for yourself. Heaven is also where you become a creator of your own reality. Your thoughts are what create a personal heaven; you can be old or young; it is up to you. This is why we hear about people seeing their relatives in heaven looking so young. We as physical beings are so limited by having a physical body but when we are in spirit form, we have the whole universe at our beck and call. If we are able to create our own piece of Heaven, then there are no limitations on what our imagination can create for us.

I do call myself a Christian because I believe in Jesus's teachings, but I am not a religious person. I am Spiritual, meaning that as a spiritual person I believe in God and seek a closer understanding of the meaning of life and to be one with the universe.

Sadly, it seems that for some being a spiritual person is just not enough because there is still to this day Christian persecution of psychics and mediums in the form of people who recite scriptures that point to the work of a medium as being the work of the devil. I will go into more detail later in this book, but for now bear in mind that the bible was written by men.

Throughout centuries the bible has been rewritten by kings and religious leaders to benefit the supremacy of the monarchy and give power to the clergy, meaning the bible as it is written today has been changed from its original content. Evidence through the discovery of the Dead Sea Scrolls, including 19 copies of the Book of Isaiah, 25 copies of Deuteronomy and 30 copies of the Psalms, indicates that the bible in its present form is not an exact record of the original content. In time, as the scholars analyze and interpret the Hebrew writings, we will know more of the truth of the original contents that were removed and changed in the modern day bible.

I decided to write this book to share what I have learned through my mediumship and to provide clarity about what Heaven is and where it is. I will be sharing descriptive stories of readings I have done throughout the years so that you may also witness how communicating with your loved ones can be very healing to the soul as well and how it can provide closure in your life.

Having a better understanding about the transitions of the soul into heaven and how the soul is affected by the way it passed away can't help but enhance the quality of how we live our lives. We will explore Christian beliefs that were written about psychics and mediums. We will learn about the Soul Family and how reincarnation plays its part.

Most importantly it is my sincerest hope that readers of this book will learn to acknowledge that Heaven is only a breath away and that our loved ones are omnipresent in our lives. You don't have to be a medium to speak to Heaven; everyone can do this. We must first learn, however, to let go of the fears and doubts that limit us. Please join me as we continue on this amazing journey of life and learn to open ourselves up to the gifts of love and healing that Heaven wishes to send to us.

Joseph LoBrutto III
(Palm Beach – 2016)

Becoming a Medium

Chapter One

I was born to parents of Italian and Spanish descent in Oceanside, New York, on an early morning in July. Yes, I am a medium who is originally from Long Island. I'm always joking that there must be something in the water there because there are a lot of great mediums from Long Island! I thought I was a normal child growing up, but when I reflect back on it, I realize that maybe I wasn't really quite your ordinary child after all. I remember attending church with my parents and the excitement for me was after church when I would shop the church sales of religious merchandise. I would spend my allowance on buying small figures of saints. When you think about it, what normal kid does that? I had a huge collection and I would place them along the windowsills in my room. I was reminded of this when I saw the movie "*Sixth Sense*" where the little boy who could see dead people would line up his saints as protection from the ghosts that were haunting him.

Like the little boy in the movie, I could see dead people. As a child I saw spirits, but to me they looked like regular people and not like the Hollywood fiction versions of gruesomeness and gore. They would talk with me and make me laugh or just pass through my room smiling. My Spirit Guides of the Collective would visit me as well. (You can read more about them in my first book ***Is There More To Life Than What We Know?***.) The daytime visits from spirits were fine, but it was the nighttime visits that scared me. I would awaken in the night to the sight of glowing white lights hovering all over my room! I began to sleep with the lights on and with my head underneath the covers in order not to see them. In time I grew older and the visions of the spirits began to fade away in my life.

My parents and my paternal grandmother, Jenny, decided to make the move from Long Island to West Palm Beach, Florida, and life was good. I grew up as a normal boy, fishing on our lake and playing baseball and basketball in the Palm Springs league. Then when I was around the age of 10 my grandmother Jenny passed away. I remember waking up in the early morning hours just before sunrise to the sound of sirens and the sight of flashing lights. I looked out my bedroom window and watched as paramedics unloaded a stretcher and minutes later they returned carrying the stretcher laden with a silent, still form – that of my grandmother - with my father Joe following closely behind. My mother, Carmen, came to me to tell me that my grandmother had passed away.

My grandmother's passing was very hard on my father. It was the first time I had ever seen him cry so hard. I can remember him saying that he had lost all faith in God because of his mother's death. That was frightening for me as a child because God had always been very important to my father.

We attended my grandmother's funeral. I had been to funerals as a younger child but I had only thought of them as a chance to see my cousins. We would usually go outside to play. I was too young at the time to understand the concepts of grieving and showing respect. It was different at my grandmother's funeral; I was now old enough to understand death and I was much closer to my grandmother, so I attended the actual service. I clearly remember how my father held my hand as we walked to the coffin and looked upon her lifeless body. "Now is the time to say our goodbyes because she is in heaven with your grandfather," my father told me. So I said my goodbyes thinking that would be the last time I would ever see my grandmother. As it turned out for me, that actually was not quite a final good-bye.

A few days later as I turned the corner into my bedroom I stopped in my tracks. I couldn't believe what I was seeing; how could this be? My grandmother Jenny was sitting on the edge of my bed smiling at me. I began shaking hard. I had no idea of what to say as my grandmother continued to sit there silently smiling. I had seen her at her funeral, I had been there when they lowered her body into the ground, and I understood that she had died – so how could she now be in my room? My dad had told me that she would be in heaven with the angels and we would not see her again! As those thoughts entered my mind, I quickly turned around and ran out of my room, but I could hear my grandmother's voice in the background saying, *"Joey, I didn't have a chance to say goodbye. I love you!"* Those words "I love you" as they were spoken to me on the day that I saw the spirit of my grandmother will forever stay in my mind. Things were quiet for a while after that. Spirits or ghosts did not appear to me throughout my childhood and teen years after the appearance of my grandmother. It wasn't until I was in my early twenties that I tapped into a great force from the universe directing me on to my incredible spiritual journey.

It all began when a friend invited me to a psychic party. Like most men I had absolutely no desire to be there. I was hugely skeptical of anyone claiming to be psychic but I went anyway. I listened to Carol, the psychic, give readings to everyone about their careers, love lives, and health as she made her rounds to all of the eager women wanting readings.

Then she approached me and said. "You have many loved ones in spirit surrounding you; they are talking your ears off and you're not listening! From their appearance, there are many generations here. They are telling me that they were psychics, mediums and healers who are your ancestors. They also tell me that you yourself have a gift and you must become open to it!" Privately I thought that this woman had to be crazy. Me, a psychic? I wanted to laugh out loud but I managed to control myself.

When she went home I thought that was the last I would see of her but I was wrong! My friend had a little surprise for me; she had signed us up for a psychic development class with Carol. I went kicking and screaming because I did not want to go. I had no idea what to expect; I actually thought I was going to be greeted by people who were dressed in robes and turbans but when I arrived, everyone was quite friendly and normal. I settled in and found myself really enjoying the class. We learned ESP techniques like how to send messages mentally and color sensing and object sensing with psychometry. Psychometry is the ability to divine information about people or events associated with an object solely by touching or being near the object. It turned out that I excelled in this exercise.

I would hold an object that belonged to someone in the group and I would be able to read amazing details about their life. I was so good at this that I quickly had a small group of people surrounding me so that they could be read. Carol pushed her way back to me through the crowd pointing a finger at me with a smile and saying, " I told you so! I told you that you were psychic!"
My curiosity was aroused. I called my mother the next day and told her about the psychic classes I was attending. I told her what the psychic had told me, that I was a psychic and that it was in my DNA. "Is this true?" I asked her.

"Joey, Joey, Joey…you were born here in America and you only know your father's side of the family. If you had ever taken the time to ask about the Puerto Rican side of your family you would have known that my brother - your uncle Jose - is a very good psychic. He told me when you were born that you would have the gift too!

"Another time my sister - your Aunt Elisa - went into trance and a male voice spoke through her talking about how one day you would make a big impact on the world when you came into your abilities. When I was a child my grandmother Francesca, who is your great-grandmother, would hold séances in her home. Hundreds of people would come to see her seeking direction in life and she would also do healings on people. This is who your family is, my son; you must embrace your calling. Don't be afraid. This is why you inherited your gifts."

So I surrendered myself to the universe and began to embrace my destiny. I read books and learned all I could about Metaphysical Science. This is when I began to communicate with my spirit guides, learning the meaning of life and channeling the writings for my first book. During the beginning years of channeling my Spirit Guides, whom I call "The Collective", my cousin Joey and his wife Marylou were very interested in the channeling of my guides.
I shared channeled messages with them about topics like why we are here, who God is, and why life can be so hard. It was during this time that my cousin Joey suddenly passed away from a heart attack. He was 34 years old, only a few years older than I was at the time. It was my cousin Joey to whom I give credit for opening the doors for me in becoming a medium. He set my spiritual journey in motion.

Speaking to Heaven Story
My Cousin Joey

It was an autumn day in mid-October when I received a phone call from my cousin Sandra telling me that her brother, my cousin Joey, had died of a heart attack that day. His sudden death was a shock to us all. How could someone so young with no health issues suddenly die of a heart attack? A few days later I attended his funeral and served as a pallbearer. As I was driving home afterwards I asked God why life was so unfair. Here was a happily married father of two young boys taken by a disease that normally only strikes older men.

As I was deep in my thoughts waiting for the light to turn green, I heard a voice out of nowhere say to me, "Hello, Joseph! I don't feel it's quite yet my time yet to go. Can we talk?" Oh, my God!!!! It was lucky that I had been at a stoplight; I would have wrecked my car if I had been moving! I thought I was losing it. Sitting next to me in the passenger seat was my cousin Joey!

He had come to ask me if I would go to Marylou and give her a message from him, but he wanted to give her the message himself. You see, I had begun channeling around this time of my life, meaning that my Spirit Guides would merge with me so they could speak through my voice and teach words of wisdom. What my cousin Joey wanted to do was like in the movie *"Ghost"* when Patrick Swayze's character, the deceased Sam who was now in spirit, wanted to jump into the body of Whoopi Goldberg's character Ode Mae, a medium, in order to dance with his wife Molly, played by Demi Moore.

Joey was asking me if he could talk to his wife by using my voice! I wanted more proof that it wasn't just my imagination, but my cousin just faded away. I decided to wait a few days to think about what had happened. Had it just been my imagination? I asked myself if maybe this was just part of the grieving process. Well, days later my cousin Joey visited me again. This time I was watching television and he appeared sitting next to me on my couch. *"Well, Joseph, are you going to let me say good goodbye to Marylou? She sits at home staring at my photo, crying on my pillow, and waiting for some kind of sign from me!"*

"Oh, boy," I thought to myself, "This is for real!" I realized I would need to make an attempt to speak with my cousin's widow. In order to obtain validation I would have to ask Joey to tell me something that only he and Marylou would know about. "What was a pet name you called her?" I asked. He thought a moment and said, *"Joseph, all you have to say is 'cheese' and she will know it's me."*

"Cheese? You've got to be kidding me, of all things you could have called her, and you are telling me you called her cheese! But OK, Joey, I'll do it." I called Marylou and arranged to see her the very next day.

I actually had to work up courage to visit Marylou and to tell her that I thought her husband Joey had visited me after his funeral. After all, she was a grieving widow; how could I be so insensitive as to tell her this when it might all be in my head? She knew that I had been channeling my guides; she had participated in many of my channeling sessions. But this was different. Suddenly I was becoming a medium? I would be asking her to take quite a leap of faith.

When she answered her door she embraced me with a hug and wept in my arms. She spoke of her anger at the unfairness of this loss and her worry that she would not be able to raise their children on her own. "Why did he leave me? I love him so much!"

I asked Marylou to have a seat and told her that I had something to tell her. I reminded her about the channeling work that she had witnessed where my spirit guides merged with me, even to the extent that I would pick up their mannerisms and personalities as they spoke through me.

After seeing the confused look on her face, I decided to get to the point. I asked her, "Do you think spirits of passed-over loved ones can do this as well?" Tears sprang to her eyes as she asked me, "What are you trying to tell me, Joseph?"

I hesitated for a moment, but then I felt the presence of Joey in the room. Now I knew there would be no getting out of this; he would haunt me forever if I didn't deliver his message! "Marylou, I will start at the beginning on the day of Joeys funeral." So I told her about the first encounter I had with Joey as I was driving home, but how I had thought it was my imagination so I put it to rest. Then I described the second encounter on the previous night as I was watching television and Joey had appeared to me again. I told her that is why I had called to meet with her.

"Marylou, did Joey call you 'cheese' as a pet name?" The expression that appeared on her face was of amazement and utter disbelief. Marylou could no longer fight back her tears. "Are you kidding me?" she exclaimed. "How do you know that?" I asked her to please confirm that Joey had called her cheese. By way of an answer, she ran to her bedroom and brought out a box full of anniversary cards, birthday cards, and love letters.

She began to open the cards and letters and on each one I saw the word 'cheese' written. Wow! I begged her to tell me what the word 'cheese' had meant to them. She paused and then started to laugh, "Well, Joseph, I wish I could tell you, but it's a personal thing between my husband and me and you will never know!"

To this day she still won't tell me what the reference to the word 'cheese' means, but that doesn't matter. What's important is that I was able to relay the message that Joey needed to tell his wife. Marylou received so much closure knowing that Joey was near. She has often met with me throughout the years since to talk with her husband. In the meantime, my cousin Joey had opened Heaven's Gates for me so that I would be able to realize my gift of seeing and communicating with the spirits of deceased loved ones. I'm always joking about how my my cousin Joey doing a 'Whoopi' on me set my mediunship abilities into motion.

Once the door was opened, it quickly became overwhelming. In fact, it was getting out of control. Everywhere I went there would be a parade of spirits wanting to talk with their loved ones. At the grocery store there would be spirits following people through the aisle. On the streets there would be spirits standing near their loved ones. I had to do something to have more control; it was very draining always having spirits approach me. I got to the point where I did not want to leave my house. I called my channeling mentor, Marilyn, and updated her about having moved into my medium abilities. "The only problem is, it's driving me crazy - it's too much!" I told her.

Marilyn suggested that I come up with a method that would open me up and another one that would shut me down. Great idea! Remember the television show starring the famous psychic medium Lisa Williams? When she was 'off duty' from spirit communication she would put on her hat and was thereby able to shut down. So what could I do?

I pondered this for days. It was late one night as I watched the movie *"Beetlejuice"* that I came up with the idea of how to open and close my connection to spirit. As I watched the part in the movie where they were supposed to say his name three times for him to appear - "Beetlejuice, Beetlejuice, Beetlejuice" - it came to me.

I would have everyone say their own name three times. In a group reading I would have everyone count from 1 to10 and then say their own name three times. When I was ready to close, I would thank everyone and say my blessings to shut down. It worked! I'm in control now; I know when spirit will show and they leave when I say goodbye. Hallelujah! By the way, you should see how excited everyone in my galleries get *on both sides* when I have a room full of people counting and saying their names at the same time!

Speaking to Heaven Story
At the Roadhouse

I was out with a friend for dinner at a local Roadhouse Grill when a server came to our table with her mother in spirit behind her, begging me to talk to her daughter. I told my friend about the server's mother in spirit and my friend began to insist that I tell her. This was at a time of my life when I was still very private in telling people that I was a medium. Mediumship was not as open as it is today. Since that time a number of television shows have showcased the work of mediums and people have become more educated that medium readings can be a cool thing and not scary. But in those days I was somewhat reluctant, so I hesitated to say anything.

However in this case my hesitation was soon over-ruled. When the server returned with our drinks, my friend said to her, "Joe here is a medium! He tells me that there is a woman in spirit who wants to tell you something important!" Oh, boy! Now the cat was out of the bag; I would have to tell this young girl about her mother.

I had her attention, so I told her, "There is a woman here who says she is your mother. Is it true that your mom passed away?" She replied with a slow and reluctant yes. "Your mother is saying that you are not doing what you are supposed to be doing. She tells me that you dropped out of nursing school!" The girl jerked back as if struck and said, "How did you know that?" My friend was laughing out loud. "I told you, he is a medium!"

Now the young girl asked me what her mother wanted. I said. "Your mother wants you to go back to school. You dropped out after her death and have been lost without her. She said you had worked so hard and you only have a year to finish. She says this was your dream. Please do it for her – and do it for yourself!" To make a long story short, I ran into that server a few weeks later and she told me that she had enrolled back in school for the fall. She wanted to make her mother proud!

In the early stages of my medium work I would do private readings in my home, improving day by day with my accuracy. It was a word-of-mouth hobby that I never would have imagined that I would do for a living. The number of readings grew as the months went by and it became overwhelming to reserve reading time for each individual person. That's when I decided to do the "John Edward style" of gallery readings where I would read to an entire audience in one sitting.

It started with small groups of six to ten people that I found very manageable, but as I grew in strength in my readings, the crowds got larger. People were inviting their friends and family to join them. One night I had around seventy-five people trying to fit into my small living room! That is when I decided to take a break, finish writing my first book and practice only my channeling. When ***"Is There More to Life Than What We Know?"*** was published, it made its way to a company called *Medium Channel* based in Germany. *Medium Channel* tests mediums from all around the world anonymously. They found me by reading my book and thought I would be a great candidate to test. They did a write up about that reading that I would love to share.

Speaking to Heaven Story
Medium Channel Reading

"Joseph calls himself a psychic medium and structures his readings so that you get the benefit of all of his polished abilities. He proved over and over during the course of my sitting that he was making a strong connection to the other side. He told me about incidents in my life with extreme accuracy. I didn't want to hang up the phone with him!

"The reading with this medium started a little differently than most. Joseph said that he makes a connection through the sound of your voice. Once I counted to ten out loud and said my name three times, we were connected and off and running. Joseph first started my reading by giving details about my personality. He connects with his guides called 'The Collective' and they in turn connect to my guides who then all have a conversation about me!

"They told him everything. After he embarrassed me with all of the details, he told me that he sees me working in a government type of office setting; he elaborated by telling me that I do work in the computer field, and was a designer. That is all correct, I am a contractor working in a government office as a system administrator/ webmaster. Joseph brought forth an unbelievable amount of information to me. He also brought through my grandmother, great grandmother, and grandfather on my dad's side. My jaw dropped when he described in the vision that he was having how I was healed at a young age and I was amazed when he described my mother's experience with a ghost.

"Next my grandmother (on my mom's side) came through. She is always the first to come and talk to me when I do a sitting. Joseph's description of my grandmother was very accurate. He said the connection is from my mother's side. He said my great-grandmother was a medium and a healer and my mother is also intuitive as well. He kept mentioning, 'Hershey'; he said this sometimes means Pennsylvania. She is from Pennsylvania and one of my clearest memories of her is when I was young when we went to Hershey Park.

"Joseph then told me that she was showing him a deck of cards and asked if this meant anything. Card playing was my grandmother's favorite pastime. Joseph said that my grandmother was here with me quite a bit, that she was acting as a guide for me. My great-grandmother (the healer) was also with me. When we started talking about her, he said he saw me as a boy looking at my hands. He said I had some kind of bumps and then he saw an eraser wipe them away and they were just gone! He asked me if this meant anything to me. It did. When I was a boy, I had warts all over my hands and feet. Basically after years of plastic surgeons and doctors trying to remove them, my great grandmother healed me with a potato and some "secret words". The warts disappeared in about a week!

"One of the most amazing things Joseph picked up on was an experience that my mother (the closet medium) had with an Amish Ghost. He said, "Your grandmother is laughing and pointing at an Amish woman. Does this mean anything to you? Yup, it sure did. She was referring to a time when my mother had seen the ghost of an Amish woman in a hotel. It almost scared her to death. I believe Joseph is one of the best psychic mediums that I have tested and his abilities are truly amazing."

Paolo~ Medium Channel.

'Medium Channel' put me on the map. My phone began to ring from all over the country and within two years I decided to retire from my video production business to become a full-time Psychic Medium. Throughout the years I have received awards and I am listed as one of the Top 100 Psychics in America. Major television networks and numerous radio shows have interviewed me. Articles have been written about my work in newspapers and magazines.

In 2012 it all shifted again. I had the opportunity to visit Brazil to meet John of God and he informed me that I would be coming into my healing abilities. I would write more about this incredible journey in future books. Today I'm known as a Spiritual Healing Medium working in the same vibration as that of John of God. Many have experienced the miraculous healing of major diseases, emotional and physical traumas, depression, and addictions and have received spiritual balance for a healthy mind, body, and soul through my divine healing service.

Is There A Heaven?

Chapter Two

I am frequently asked about one of life's biggest mysteries – heaven. What is heaven and where is it and is there a hell? People who have had a near death experience usually describe entering a bright white tunnel only to be turned back. Could this be the entrance of heaven? There has been much written about heaven, from fluffy white clouds to the heavenly gates of Saint Peter. There is a movie about heaven and the afterlife that really stands out for me as depicting quite accurately heaven as it has been described to me by my spirit guides of the 'Collective'. It's called *"What Dreams May Come"* starring the late Robin Williams (may God bless his soul and help him heal his pain).

The movie was released in 1998 and classified as "fantasy drama", but I believe this movie is far from being fantasy. I think it is a true depiction of heaven. In the movie Chris Nielsen (Robin Williams) dies in a car accident and is guided through the afterlife by his spirit guide, Doc Albert (Cuba Gooding Jr.). His new world is beautiful and can be whatever Chris imagines. Even his children, who were also killed in an auto accident years before, are there in their own beautifully created worlds.

When his wife Annie (Annabelle Sciorra) commits suicide, her afterlife is a vision of hell. Chris ignores Albert's warnings and journeys there to save her. Upon his arrival, Chris finds that rescuing Annie will be more difficult than he'd imagined.

I had gone with a friend to see "*What Dreams May Come*" when it was released in the theaters. My friend was lost throughout much of the movie and I noticed other people in the theater were also shaking their heads in confusion. In the meantime, because of my unique perspective as a channel, I was excited about how everything was depicted in the movie because I had an idea of heaven and the afterlife from my guides' descriptions.

Based on our current cultural perspective I can see how people might have been confused if they weren't looking at the movie from a metaphysical point of view. In this chapter I'm going to use some scenes from the movie that I feel are relevant to explaining the concepts of heaven and hell and what our loved ones are doing in heaven. But first let me paint a picture of how the movie unfolds.

What Dreams May Come
Wedding and a Funeral

Chris and Annie meet on a lake in Switzerland when Annie's small sailboat approaches Chris' rowboat and she asks him for directions. A few hours later they run into each other on land. She offers Chris half of her sandwich and it's love at first bite. Years later they are married with two children and we come to a scene where the family is in their kitchen having breakfast. Annie, an art curator, is running late for work that morning and asks the home caretaker if she would drive the children to school. It is the last time that Chris and Annie ever see their children alive; tragically they are involved in a car accident and they are killed.

Annie blames herself. She believes that if she had driven the kids to school her motherly instincts would have kept her children out of harm's way. Chris, who had studied psychology before becoming a pediatric physician, provides the strength for Annie to keep going and is able to save her when she tries to commit suicide. Time passes and life goes on. One day Annie, who is an artist as well as an art curator, calls Chris at his practice with a dilemma.

Some of the featured art pieces have not arrived for that evening's art exhibit. Chris offers to go pick up the paintings but he does not make it. On the way there he is involved in an accident with a number cars in one of the city's tunnels. The scene shows Chris muddled and confused lying on the pavement and a voice is asking him if he realizes what has happened to him.

Chris replies with a joke about how he must be hallucinating. Barely alive, he is transported by ambulance as the paramedics employ every measure to resuscitate him. While he is in the emergency room hooked to life support he hears the voice again talking to him, telling him that it's time to let go as the heart monitor begins to flat line.

Chris suddenly finds himself in front of his house. The family dog barks happily and runs toward him with his tail wagging, but we soon realize that no one else can see him. We now flash forward a few days as Chris appears in the living room of his home filled with grieving mourners. He is saddened to see Annie on the couch surrounded by friends trying to comfort her as she stares at a painting she had done of Chris standing by a tall willow tree.

As Chris is watching these events, including his own funeral, he continually hears a voice asking him if he understands what has happened to him. Chris now sees an image with the voice, but it's blurred and the voice explains that this is because Chris has not fully accepted the fact of his own death. He tells Chris that he is Doc Albert, an old friend and mentor to Chris, and that he is there to help guide Chris through the transition of his death.

Doc Albert advises Chris that it's time for him to move on, but Chris refuses to go and insists that he is not leaving Annie. For a time Chris pursues Annie persistently hoping that she will be able to sense that he is there. Doc warns Chris that he has to leave Annie alone and explains that she needs to be able to grieve; that Chris is only hurting her by sticking around. The last attempt that Chris makes is a few weeks later when Annie visits his grave. Chris approaches her and tries to wrap his arms around her and whisper words of endearment, but Annie begins to shake with fear and to cry. Chris backs off, realizing that Doc Albert was right. Annie then feels a sense of release and knows that Chris has moved on.

Spiritual Guides

Let's go back to Chris's car accident when he first hears the voice of his mentor and friend, Doc Albert. During a time of near death crossed-over family members, friends, angels and spirit guides begin to appear in order to help the dying person make their transition from the physical world into the spiritual. They are there to help the spirit to understand what is happening and to offer spiritual guidance. This can be a time of confusion for the soul because it feels that it is still a part of this earthly reality, so it drifts in and out into the higher reality called the "astral realm" where our souls go after death.

The astral realm is a plane of existence between existences; it spans the earthly and heavenly realms. The spirit is omnipresent in the astral realm, meaning it can be everywhere at once, but feels more grounded to the earthly realm because that was recently home. It's like being in a dream state. As three dimensional beings, we are vibrating at a three dimensional frequency while still in the physical body. When we die we shed our physical body and we are left with our energetic body, which is our soul. Now the soul will vibrate at a higher frequency in the astral realm and will vibrate even more intensely as it enters into the higher realm past heaven where the Angels and Ascended Masters reside.

Where is God?

You might ask where God is in all of this. Is he a man in a long, white beard as Hollywood portrays him or is he a being of pure light – or is he neither? The answer is that everything in the universe is of God. Every living thing and all that you can see is of God.

Consider our solar system with the Sun at the center of our galaxy and all of the planets rotating around it at different levels. Imagine God as the center of all soul levels; He is the Light. All souls revolve around the Light at different levels. The level closest to God is of the Ascended Masters who have reached enlightenment such as Jesus, Moses, Joshua, and Buddha. The Archangels and the entire band of angels reside on the next level, followed by the souls of others in higher dimensions than Earth (think in terms of enlightened extraterrestrials). The next level is heaven; this is only a shadow of the earth; then comes the human race on earth.

Transitioning after Death

Have you ever heard the phrase 'we are spiritual beings having a human experience'? Our life here on earth is very short. Heaven is where our soul will live forever. As a medium I'm able to tap into what goes on during the transition of the soul from the physical world to the spiritual. For example, sometimes the spirit will go into denial and will have trouble believing that it has died. Normally those who have had a quick and unexpected death are the ones that need time to adjust and seek answers from their spiritual guides. In life Doc Albert had been a mentor and inspiration to Chris; this is why he appeared to Chris as a spiritual guide. If you had looked at someone as an authority figure in life, then in the afterlife during the time of transition such a person might act as your guide since they would be someone that you would trust and most likely listen to. Doc Albert appeared as a blur to Chris while he was still in doubt that he had died, but when he came to terms with his death he was able to see Doc Albert clearly.

The spirit will attend its own funeral and check on their loved ones from time to time. Time does not exist in the astral realm; this is time for the spirit to adjust to the experience of being of energy rather than of substance. If it is a spouse who is in spirit, I find that the spirit will grieve as well for the love of their life. They want to do everything in their power to make their spouse know that they are still near. We are energetic beings and when we are connected at a soul level with someone, there are cords that tightly bind us together. (Soul level connection simply means the couple's connection was not merely at the level of the physical personality; it is also at the level of the soul.)

Does the spirit move on or stay?

One question I'm frequently asked is if people are holding back their loved ones when they could be enjoying heaven. Those left behind sometimes feel guilty and selfish that they are refusing to let their loved ones go. Here is where I have to disagree with the movie. Doc Albert was trying to help Chris to move on by cutting the cords from Annie that held him here on earth. As a channel I'm able to feel the emotions of the deceased person and feel their grief. The spirit must go through the emotions of dying and dealing with not being able to express themselves physically. During this transition period and time of grieving is when the spirit will be with their family.

The spirit chooses to do this; we are not holding them back. It's like having one foot in one room and the other foot in a different room; the spirit is omnipresent it can be everywhere at once. It can be days, weeks, months and sometimes years that a spirit will be earth-bound. It all depends on the needs of the spirit as to when it chooses to move toward the heavenly realm.

One sign that it is time for the spirit to move on is when the energy of the spirit becomes weak and the memory of the spirit's life on earth begins to fade; then they will have a strong desire to go into the light and their spiritual guides will direct them through to the heavenly realm. When passing through the veil, the spirit is rejuvenated with God's energy, making it free and truly bringing it home again. The spirit merges with its "oversoul" where it unites with loved ones who have passed over previously and finds a whole new world to explore. Also, the total memory of the spirit is restored and it will remember the life it once had and all of its past lives. Remember that when it is time for you to cross over, your loved ones will be waiting for you to share their life with them in heaven.

The "Oversoul" is a reflection of The God consciousness; here is where our soul is God-like. It is consciousness that includes all memories of our soul family, making the family as one. It is one soul for everyone. The "Soul Family" is the spiritual equivalent to your birth family here on earth. They may take the form of a relative here on earth, or they could be anyone in your life. When you meet them, they feel like your siblings, parents, or children. You and your soul family share the same oversoul, so you are all aspects of the same soul. The universe is constantly in a cycle of death and rebirth, with people going on to have many lives.

Losing a Spouse or Significant Other

What I find striking is how frequently there continues to be a strong soul-level connection with a spouse or significant other that is in spirit. If the living partner and their deceased loved one had a long or a strong relationship together, there will continue to be loyalty and a strong connection between them.

My cousin Marylou experienced this with her husband. She felt his presence for years and felt at peace knowing he was looking after her and the boys. Eventually there came a time when she felt that she could move on with her life and perhaps meet someone new and to find love once more. I find that our loved ones in spirit - particularly a spouse - very much want us to live our life happily and not alone, especially if you still have many years to live your life. Marylou was in her early thirties and was much too young to remain alone.

Most of the time it is even our spouse or significant other who directs the new person into our lives. When Marylou came to the point that she wanted to move forward, Joey gave her the space she needed to find love once more. That doesn't mean that she would not speak to Joey again; in fact, she already has. I know this because Marylou had a family group reading with me this past year. Her boyfriend Montgomery was there and didn't quite know what to expect since this was his first time receiving a mediumistic reading. It was a profound moment when, after I had channeled his son, father, and grandfather for him, my cousin Joey dropped in to thank him for taking care of Marylou and his boys. Both Marylou and Montgomery were in tears as they received Joey's blessings.

The Power of Love

In this day and age it is hard to find couples that met early in life who are still together into their golden years when so many first marriages end in divorce. My parents have been married for over fifty-five years; they are in their eighties and they still have a beautiful soul connection. When I see couples like this I know that there is a true soul connection. In my work I also witness how, after losing a spouse after so many years together, the surviving partner often feels it is their time to go and they frequently pass away within days, months, or a few years. This is a scenario I find many times when reading for someone who is at the end of their lifespan.

The living spouse will find that the spirit of their beloved will not move on to the heavenly realm, but rather will stand by their side to be the first to greet them after their passing. Then the couple will move into the heavenly realm together.

I had a situation recently with a persistent husband waiting to talk with his wife. He would not leave me alone all day and even disrupted earlier readings. His name, Al, came up in two earlier readings with both clients not knowing an Al. This spirit was so strong that I felt him to be more earth-bound then in the astral realm. It was driving me crazy because no one would claim him!

My last session of the day was for a group of three. When I went to greet them at the reception area, Al took over because, of course, it was Al's widowed wife and two adult children who had come for a reading. Finally! The wife got up from her chair to greet me and as she did so Al spoke through me declaring, "*It's me, Al!*" She fell back to the chair in surprised disbelief. I apologized and explained that a spirit named Al had been trying to connect with me all day waiting for her. This time there was plenty of validation for Al.

During the reading Al talked about an old Model T Ford they had owned. The son confirmed this. "He had me crank the car to start it! It was a car he presented at car shows," he said. Al had some messages for his son. "Your father wants you to remember the time you went fishing for flounder in the bay when you were a child. He's also speaking of the first Yankee game he took you to."

Next I addressed the daughter, but again Al spoke through me. "*I see you are wearing my ring around your neck*," he said and with tears in her eyes she pulled out his alumni ring from under her shirt. Al now addressed his wife. "*I have been by your side every day since my passing. Darling, heaven is not heaven without you! I promise to wait for you.*" I wanted to share this story because it shows how strong and loving a relationship can be even beyond death and how persistent our loved ones on the other side are in wanting to let us know that they still exist and they are not far away.

What Dreams May Come
Is This Heaven?

As we return to our movie we can observe how Chris begins to experience heaven. At first after passing Chris feels a pull that draws him toward a brightly lit tunnel. As he travels through the tunnel he sees forms of other people being guided through and the scene fades to white. He wakes up in a field of flowers with his face on the ground. He gets up slowly and begins to wipe what he thinks is dirt from his face, but on closer inspection he can see that it is acrylic paint. He looks around at the vivid colors of the grass and trees and wonders if he is dreaming. He makes his way toward a cliff overlooking a lake when he sees something familiar. Just on the other side of the lake is the willow tree that Annie painted. Laughing, he exclaims *"Annie! It is so beautiful!"*

Doc Albert appears and Chris admires all of the beautiful scenery. Doc Albert assures him that it was all actually created by Chris; that he loved Annie's painting so much that he created his heaven as one of her paintings. Likewise, Doc Albert does not look old as he did at the end of his life, but has chosen to appear to Chris as a young man. They discuss the metaphysics of a heaven that we create with thoughts, because as Doc Albert explains, *"Thought is what is real, and your thoughts are your creations."*

Welcome to Heaven

There have been many stories of people who had a near death experience that have reported seeing a bright white light at the end of a tunnel. Others experience a feeling of utter peace. Some encounter an unfamiliar person who was there to guide them while others found crossed-over relatives awaiting them as guides. But what comes next? Is there a heaven?

In my line of work I'm often asked what heaven is and what do our loved ones do in heaven. I tell them heaven can be anything they want it to be. Heaven is also called the Astral Plane; it's the place of learning. Most people believe that heaven is beyond the stars and the universe, but it is not. Heaven is within you; it's a breath away. When we whisper, our loved ones can hear us.

Like Chris in the movie, we will find that heaven is wherever or whatever we want it to be. If you feel that waterfalls, sunsets, sunrises and angels mean heaven to you, then that's the heaven you will create for yourself. Heaven is where you become a creator of your own reality. Your thoughts are what create a personal heaven; you can be old or young; it will be up to you. This is why we hear about people seeing their relatives in heaven looking young. As physical beings we are limited by having a physical body but when we are in spirit form we have the whole universe at our front door. There are no limitations on what our imagination can create for us.

Life in Heaven

People also inquire about what our loved ones are doing in heaven. To fully appreciate the answer we must stop thinking in terms of three dimensional reality. The soul must go through its transition from being a physical being to a spiritual being by experiencing different levels in order to progress to its full potential. These are the levels of progression:

Level One - Adjustment Period and Fantasy Land
Level Two - Reuniting with Family
Level Three - Reincarnation
Level Four - Assignments in Heaven (If the soul chooses not to reincarnate)

Level One - Adjustment Period and Fantasy Land

Just think if we could create anything at all through our own thoughts; imagine what we would create for ourselves by simply using our imagination! When we die we shed our physical body and return to our true spiritual form and we learn (or remember how) to do exactly that. Once more we become a very powerful consciousness that holds the knowledge of the universe. With one thought we can create whatever we want and need.

When the soul first passes through the veil into the heavenly realm, its memories of its most recent life on earth as well as past lives are also restored. I call this the adjustment period and the reality of the soul becomes “fantasy land”. The soul will create for itself an environment of enjoyment, pleasure, and peace. The soul will reminisce about what they loved about life on the earth and replicate it as their heaven. There is no time in this reality so the soul will rest and wait for returning soul family members while enjoying their heavenly peace.

Level Two - Reuniting with the Soul Family

In the marriage vows we often hear the phrase “until death us do part”. Does death actually part us? In a physical sense, yes, death separates us but in a spiritual sense, no, we will always be together. It is because we are part of the same soul family. A soul family is made up of any number of individual souls who regularly incarnate at the same time. This is our soul family to whom we are spiritually connected; these are souls we’re meant to connect with in both the spirit world and here by choice in physical form. We may or may not be physically related to them in our current lifetime.

People from our soul family come into our lives during random times and sometimes even in unpleasant ways. Before we were born we agreed to connect and teach one another lessons in this lifetime. People in our soul family are friends, siblings, parents, family, lovers and even coworkers. This explains why some people are only in our lives for a short time just to make a profound impact while others are with us much longer.

Recognizing Souls from our Soul Family

Here are some ways that you may recognize people from your soul family.

- You may recognize their energy right away; it may feel like you have known that person all of your life.
- You may feel like you have met somewhere before, but can't remember where or when.
- You feel an emotional attraction towards the person that surpasses any emotional connection you could have built with them in the time period you've known them.
- You both have a distinctive awareness that you are going through something important together that will leave you feeling more spiritually aware.

Speaking to Heaven Story
Melissa's Soul Family

I was invited to a home in Stuart, Florida, to facilitate a "Speaking to Heaven Gallery". The hostess, Melissa, had endured losing so many family members in her lifetime that she wanted to make sure that they were fine and all together. I began the gallery with a married couple who are good friends with Melissa. I felt that they had a daughter in spirit. When she came through I felt her hesitation to speak and my throat began to close, making it hard for me to breathe. I felt my heart racing as I was trying to pull myself together. Then she spoke through me: *"I am so sorry, I have hurt you both. Please forgive me!"*

The room was still as these words came out of my mouth and . everyone was wondering what would come next. *"I was so depressed about everything in life that I did not want to deal with it anymore. That is why I took my life."* Both parents were speechless and I could sense the pain they carried with them.

"Your daughter would like me to elaborate on her message to you," I said. "She says that you are beautiful parents and you had tried everything in your power to help her with her suicidal issues. It was not your fault; she is taking full responsibility about her death. She is asking you, *'Please forgive me!'"* They were beside themselves but they needed to hear those words from their daughter. It gave them a sense of peace and closure knowing that their daughter was in a peaceful place and they had validation that they had done everything that they could to help her.

Melissa was in tears as my attention was now drawn to her and her daughter. I said "I have a young boy here that has a 'J' in his name". Melissa said, "I believe it's my son, J.T."

"Next he is showing me a vision of the universe. I'm looking into the sky and I can see the stars and planets, but they are not far away; it's like I can reach up and touch the stars." Now Melissa can absolutely confirm that it was J.T. She tells the group that his room would glow in the dark with the stars and planets that were glued to the ceiling. Since he was a paraplegic and spent much time in bed, he would stare for hours at the ceiling filled with stars.

Then I felt a big shift of energy; it felt more feminine, like a mother figure. "I have someone named Mary; she tells me she is your mother and is watching over J.T. You prayed that she would be there for J.T. Your mother wants to let you know he is safe with her. Days before J.T.'s passing he sensed your mother around him; J.T. knew how to find her. But Melissa, your mother is concerned about your heath; cancer is the culprit in many deaths in the family. She says that you are sick as well, is this is true?"

Melissa responded that yes, she did have cancer and it was in its final stages. "I'm not afraid of death but I worry about leaving my daughter behind. What gives me peace is that she has a great relationship with her father, my ex-husband, and he will take care of her." Melissa's soul family in spirit was growing larger than the family members who were alive.

Later, Melissa gave me feedback for the gallery.

"Once again Joseph, you prove yourself to be AMAZING. Friday night's gallery was really special. Not only did I receive several messages, but just the experience of watching you put so many people's minds and hearts at ease by letting them communicate with loved ones they have lost and miss terribly always leaves me in AWE of you.

For someone like me who has lost so many, your galleries are far superior to any grief counseling. You give me vast hope and a bit of peace with the knowledge that my loved ones are not only fine, but also incredibly happy and thriving on the other side. The details that come out of your mouth are amazing...Thank you, THANK YOU from the bottom of my heart." - Melissa Y

Melissa was one of the strongest people that I have met; I regret to say that she passed away months later, joining her son J.T and the rest of her soul family. May you rest in peace Melissa - love to you.

Level Three - Reincarnation

Reincarnation is the belief that a soul is born multiple times into new bodies throughout time. The soul travels on an eternal path living in one body for a time, dying, and then entering a new body to live again. The purpose of reincarnation is to serve out karma from previous lives and thus eventually reach a state of perfect enlightenment where additional human lives are no longer necessary.

I'm often asked about reincarnation during my sessions. Most people want to know if their loved ones will come back to the family as one of their children or grandchildren. They also wonder how they will be able to contact them in spirit if they are not in heaven anymore.

A high percentage of souls do journey back to the earth realm when they feel it's time to continue soul growth. When the soul decides to reincarnate it will choose an infant from its soul family in which to be born. When the baby takes its first breath, the soul enters into the infant's body. It now has a new identity, soul purpose, and life. The memory of its last incarnation begins to fade as it begins its new life journey. Now you may be thinking, OK, the soul is here on earth; so how is a medium going to contact my loved one on the other side? Again, we must stop thinking in three dimensional terms!

Let's think of heaven as our oversoul where our soul family consciousness is collected. Think of the oversoul as a "hard drive." The hard drive will hold all of the essence and memories of your entire ancestry of your soul family. When the soul decides to reincarnate, the soul will travel away from the oversoul (hard drive) to live its life as a physical being. Even when the soul becomes a physical being it cannot be separated from the oversoul. Think of it as a bluetooth or a wireless connection without any loss of service - you're always connected! In a reading the medium will tap into the oversoul/hard drive that contains all of the consciousness of your soul families with all of the memories intact of the person you want to contact, even when the soul has reincarnated into another member of the soul family.

If reincarnation is real, then how can the population be so much larger now than in the past? How can there be so many more people on the planet today than before? One reason is based on the frequency of incarnation. In the past the population on Earth was much smaller so souls could incarnate much less frequently. This was during a time when people lived well into their hundreds. In past eras a soul may have only been able to incarnate once every thousand years, but when the population grew ten times larger over time, a soul could then incarnate every hundred years. With today's population, it appears that souls can incarnate almost continually.

Another possibility, with the population growth, is that other beings from other dimension besides three dimensional earth may have a desire to experience life as a three dimensional being and now have an opportunity to do so. The universe is grand; it's hard to imagine that the human race of earth is the only creation of God!

Birth of a Soul

Your oversoul that houses your soul family has been evolving for millions of years. It grows and learns by having karmic lessons from experiences of your soul family.

In the beginning your soul is a vibration of devotion and privilege. It is a form of God that is created in his own image. But how is one to grow spiritually when one's true 'being-ness' of Light is already of pure love? That is why the earth was created; it was made as a schoolhouse of karmic growth for the soul to learn and grow.

A note on Karma: For every action there will always be a reaction. Your thoughts and actions are powerful. They carry energy. They are like an echo. We have all taken a different path in life but somehow we are all linked. Whatever you do will always come back to you.

In order for the soul to learn and grow it has to experience life on the earth where it can experience love, peace, adversity, sorrow, misery, devotion, tranquility and contentment. The teachings of Kabbalah (Jewish Mysticism) explain that the creator takes a soul and splits it into two, causing the masculine and feminine energies. Then it's split into many smaller pieces creating multiple masculine and feminine energies, making it into many soul families.

This all happens before the soul is cast into human form. As a soul we have had many incarnations on earth sharing our love with many other souls that are a part of our soul's family. Your lovers in this lifetime were also your lovers in a past lifetime.

Your mother might have been your sister; your father might have been your brother. This is the concept of having a soul family where you can change roles and learn from each other through the passing of time.

Past Lives

I recommend Dr. Brian Weiss' book, *"Many Lives, Many Masters"*, where he describes sessions of past-life hypnosis with his patients that show how our soul can live many lives. Past life memories are the autobiography of your eternal soul; they are personal stories that help to explain who you are now and why you're here on Earth. We were not born with memories from past lives into this life but unconsciously, these memories often continue to affect us.

It is hard to believe that we would only have one soul and one lifetime. According to science the earth is around 4.5 billion years old. The jawbone of a human found in a South African cave may be up to 2.8 million years old. Humans began as a primitive race and in the course of millions of years they have evolved into a superior race. If we consider how the soul first incarnated into primitive man over 2.8 millions years ago, we realize that the soul had to experience an evolution as well as the human race.

Remember that the essence of the soul is God-like. When it first incarnated into a primitive human, it must have felt trapped by being in a body without a way to truly express itself. When a soul is born into a human body it will remember the presence of God. As months go by the memory of God begins to fade and the young soul is absorbed into its society of the primitive man.

During my readings and upon request I will occasionally tap into my client's past lives if I feel that it will benefit their growth as a person or their spiritual journey. Sometimes knowing one's past life may affect personal growth in this lifetime. Past memories, phobias, and fears will surface that may have been having an adverse effect on spiritual growth. I believe that the purpose of not knowing all of the details of our past lives is so that we can have personal growth without being concerned with past life events. We are to put our energy into the life we are now living instead of trying to correct something we may have done hundreds of years ago in another lifetime.

Speaking to Heaven Story
A Husband Reincarnates

Having a "Speaking to Heaven" gallery for a four-generation family was a lot of fun. They laughed, cried, and reminisced of times when everyone was alive. Debbie, the host who held the home party, introduced me to her mother and to her daughter who just had a baby boy a few months prior. A dozen other women were present as well. Everyone was excited for the chance to hear from loved ones who had passed away. The hostess of the party was very excited because she'd had a psychic reading the previous year and the psychic had told her that her grand baby was the reincarnation of her father who passed away many years ago.

Toward the end of the gallery I told Debbie that I had saved the best for last. Everyone looked at me expectantly as Debbie's daughter bounced her baby on her knee to keep him quiet. I said to Debbie, "I have someone asking about her green emerald ring. Is this your grandmother on your father's side? She wants to know if you are wearing the ring."

"Yes!" Debbie exclaimed as she pulled the ring out of her pocket and placed it on her finger to show everyone. She then explained to the group that she had told her grandmother that if I mentioned the ring, then she would know it was actually her grandmother. "But then I thought Joseph might see the ring and guess it belonged to someone in spirit, so I hid it in my pocket," she said with a laugh.

What happened next created some confusion. "I have a person who tells me that he is your father. He died of a heart attack while he was in the living room. Your mother found him sitting in his reclining chair." Debbie validated this information. "Yes, that's him; he died while watching late night TV. My mom found him when he didn't turn in for bed. But Joseph - we were so sure that he reincarnated as my grandson!" That's when the spirit of her father explained, *"Yes, my soul can incarnate into more than one body at once. My soul is omnipresent; it can be everywhere at once. Joseph is speaking to me here and a part of me is also over there as our grandson."*

Then I explained to the group about the concept of having a soul family and how the person who passed away will frequently reunite with its soul family. When the soul is ready to reincarnate for a new soul purpose, a part of the soul will make its way to a new family member who is about to be born. Debbie and her family loved that answer, and they loved knowing that the baby is a part of her father's soul.

Level Four - Assignments in Heaven

When souls are ready to accomplish something more meaningful than experiencing their "fantasy land", they will be given tasks to do that will help other souls as well as helping their own soul to grow to its full spiritual potential and enlightenment. Ultimately when the soul has graduated into a higher realm of existence - meaning it does not have to reincarnate on earth for growth anymore - it becomes an ascended being. Masters like Moses, Joshua, Buddha, and Jesus have reached such a state of enlightenment. There are many tasks given to souls throughout eternity.

Spiritual Tasks

I find throughout the course of my readings that special tasks are sometimes given to our loved ones in heaven. I was reading for a mother who lost her daughter. I asked if her daughter worked with animals or rescued them; I could see her tending to their needs. The mother responded that yes, her daughter had been studying to become a veterinarian. "Well, your daughter is telling me that she works with animals in heaven and she makes sure that tortured animals are loved." Another reading was for an older married couple that had lost their adult daughter to cancer. When she came through I felt that she was a very loving, caring soul who worked with and loved children but never had any of her own. Her life seemed empty when it came to relationships; she had been alone in her life. Her parents validated what I told them. She had been a schoolteacher in her fifties and had never married, but she would volunteer all of her free time at the children's hospital. I then added, "She is doing this as well in heaven for all of the children who were lost souls; she is there to guide them." So as you can see, there are many tasks in heaven for souls to do.

What Dreams May Come

Soul Mates

Annie blames herself for Chris's death. She believes that if she hadn't been so selfish, Chris wouldn't have gone to the warehouse the evening he died. She sits in front of a blank canvas that is part of a triptych that she had begun painting when Chris was alive. The left canvas shows a vast landscape with a blurred figure of a woman. The blurred woman represents Annie, who has lost herself; she no longer wants to exist. The center canvas shows Chris standing in awe of the magnificence of a willow tree. Annie begins to paint the last canvas; she draws a mighty tree in the foreground soaring to the very edge of the top of the canvas. She paints lavender leaves which look as if they were pouring down from the tree.

She wonders aloud if Chris can see her new painting from heaven. As she finishes painting we can see in Chris's heaven that the earth begins to quake as Annie's tree sprouts up from the ground and quickly towers up over Chris and Doc. Chris tells Doc that wasn't him; that he believes it's actually Annie. Doc is uncertain. How can one person create in the heaven of another without even being in that heaven? But then he reasons that Chris and Annie must be soul mates and that is why Annie can be a part of Chris's heaven. He says that it's rare, but it happens; twin souls can reach out to one another even after death. It seems as though they are reaching one another through Annie's painting.

Meanwhile Annie ponders her painting. Suddenly she exclaims out loud that she does not believe Chris can see her because he is dead. In her grief and anguish she grabs a bottle of paint remover and pours it all over the canvas. In the painting, the tree begins to streak and dissolve away. In Chris's heaven the tree groans as it splits in two with its now-dead leaves blowing in the wind. Chris calls out that he loves her and, appearing to have heard him, Annie looks up and wonders if those words were in her head. But soon she succumbs to her feeling that there is no more meaning in her life.

In heaven Chris can't stop thinking about Annie. Everywhere he looks he sees something that reminds him of her. Doc tells him he needs to stop thinking about her and even brings up the notion that Chris might like to see his children. Chris had been so focused on Annie that he had not yet looked for them. Now, on the ground near his feet, Chris can suddenly see a stuffed tiger that had belonged to his daughter Marie. He turns to Doc and asks where are his children, and come to think if it, why has he not seen them yet? Doc advises Chris that when he is ready to see them he will.

In the next scene Chris is surprised when a Polynesian woman dressed as a flight attendant approaches him. She introduces herself as Ariel and tells Chris she was sent to show him realities other then his own. The tour begins in a boat as they travel by river through a sunlit jungle. Ariel asks Chris if he had a special memory with his daughter. He recalls one day during a time when he had realized how busy his work had been as a pediatric doctor; it had suddenly seemed to him that he had spent more time taking care of the children who were his patients then his own kids.

One morning when Marie had not come down for breakfast he had gone upstairs to check on her. She was still in bed with a fever. Chris lets her sleep and when he checks on her a few hours later she was feeling a little better. Marie asks him if he had to be somewhere and he replies that he had taken the day off. Then he proposes a game of chess. Marie is surprised and happy at the unexpected opportunity to spend quality time with her father.

As Chris recalls the day they had spent together, he remembers in particular a large, colorful cutout she had next to her bed. It showed a building with steps leading to a pair of large doors. On the steps was a boy riding a unicycle and in the air was a woman flying through the air on a flying trapeze; everyone is dressed in clothing styles of the late nineteenth century. Marie had asked him, *"Do you think heaven is like this?"* Chris had smiled and answered, *"I don't know, honey, but it would make a wonderful heaven!"* Recalling that day with Marie playing chess makes him smile and he tells Ariel that it was a very special day for him.

The boat leaves the jungle and enters a whimsical city. It's exciting to see a place that is so different from his own heaven. The buildings soar high into a sky covered with fluffy white clouds. The sound of children's laughter fills the streets. Everyone is dressed in clothes of the late 1800's. Chris is mesmerized watching the people; when he sees a boy on a unicycle it stirs a vague memory for him, but it isn't until he sees a woman leap from a step and begin to ascend upwards by rope toward a trapeze that it occurs to him *that this was his daughter's heaven!*

Ariel takes Chris's hand and tells him a story about how when she was young her father had taken the family on vacation to Hawaii. When the flight attendant placed a lei around his neck, he had remarked how beautiful he thought Polynesian women were and she had remembered that. She tells him that is why she had chosen to look as she now did for her Daddy. Then Ariel - actually Marie - reaches out to hug her father and appears again as Marie, his little girl.

Who are our Soul mates?

I definitely believe in soul mates, but my definition extends beyond the traditional idea that we only have one soul mate in our lifetime. Another misconception about soul mates is that they have to be our lovers. In reality, a soul mate is someone we are close to at a soul level in many kinds of relationships; it can be anyone from grandparents, parents, siblings, aunts, uncles, or in-laws to best friends and of course, romantic relationships. There is a deep love for one another and a spiritual bond that sets soul mates apart from other people in our lives. Our soul mates are in our lives to help us grow spiritually; they are a part of our soul family. The soul will spend numerous lifetimes with their soul family in order for the soul to learn through karmic ties with its own soul family. In one lifetime someone might be your spouse and in the next, they might be a parent.

The reason why we share many lifetimes with the same soul family is to learn cause and effect of karma and how what comes around goes around. This is why life isn't always easy with the one you love and at times they may seem to be your worst enemy. When the lessons of karma are over with a certain individual, you can then move on to other lessons without owing that debt anymore. When you meet a soul mate that has strong karmic ties with you, they'll feel very familiar and the energy will be intense when you first meet. It will feel as if you have been together for many lifetimes - because you have! You can have many different soul mates in one life and also love the same soul mate in numerous of lifetimes.

Twin Souls

When Annie reached out to Chris through her painting Doc had observed that it was like "twin souls reaching each other even after death." Twin souls - also called twin flames - are literally the other half of our soul. When the soul is split into many smaller energies making the soul family, each one is split once again making them twins.

The twin souls go their separate ways incarnating over and over to gather human experience on the earth plane before coming back together in the spiritual realm. Unlike our soul family members who are only stepping stones to prepare the soul to meet its twin, the twin soul is the other half of our soul and meeting our twin can be the start of the ultimate relationship.

In the past it was not so common to find one's twin soul since twin souls reincarnate on the earth plane together only when it's their last incarnation on earth. This is done so they may come together to experience ascension into a higher realm of existence. Each twin must learn to become more whole, balance their female and male sides, and ideally to become enlightened before reuniting with their twin as spirit. However, nowadays more and more twins are finding one another as the earth is entering into the new age and humanity is making a big shift forward in consciousness. During the coming Age of Aquarius the acceleration of spiritual transformation along with the opportunities for soul evolution is upon us. Because of the acceleration of the planet people are evolving at a much faster rate. Some people are now learning in months what used to take a lifetime to learn. When the two halves of twin flames cross paths, they will experience a powerful cosmic bond between them because they really are of the same soul and are so very much alike that they complete one another.

Soul Family Mansions

Jesus once said that in his father's house there are many mansions. What does that actually mean? If we look at our soul, it is of pure energy. Our thoughts become our reality which in turn creates our heaven. I believe that the mansions are thoughts of souls that create their own heavens. When Chris asked to see his daughter Marie, he traveled through a jungle leaving his own mansion and found his daughter's mansion in heaven.

Chris's mansion was very different from Marie's because their thoughts of what heaven would be like were not the same. We are in control of our own mansion, but we can share our mansions with others in our soul family if we choose to do so as well as visit as many mansions as we choose.

The next part of the story from *"What Dreams May Come"* is about lost souls and hell. Here is where Hollywood takes over because knowing what I know as a medium, I realize that it doesn't happen the way that the movie portrays in regard to lost souls, suicides and Hell. I will tell the story the way it was told in the movie and then afterward I will give my view on these topics.

What Dreams May Come
The Gates of Hell

Chris feels blessed seeing his daughter Marie and now he is eager to see his son, but just then Doc Albert returns and says that he has some bad news; he tells Chris that Annie has died. Chris is naturally saddened at first, but then he thinks about how she will no longer be in pain and they will be together once more and that brings him a sense of peace. He asks Doc when he will see her but Doc has more bad news. He explains that Chris does not understand - because Annie committed suicide, he will never get to see her!

Chris becomes angry at this news, but Doc tells him that he doesn't make the rules, it's just the way things work. What some people call hell is for those who don't know they are dead. They don't realize what they have done or what is happening to them. Suicides go to hell for a different reason. Each of us has an instinct and there is a natural order to our journey. He explains that Annie violated that natural order and because she won't face it and accept what she has done she will spend eternity playing it out.

Chris is not happy with any of what Doc is telling him, but where Annie is concerned, he is determined. After some discussion Chris reasons that if he is Annie's soul mate, he should be able to find her, so Doc Albert agrees to help him and they go off to find a soul tracker who will guide them through the gates of hell. Doc and Chris set sail in a small boat to seek a tracker. They enter a city with many canals that stretch out for miles in many directions. Soon they come to a tall building housing shelves and shelves of books towering over them. This is the library of the Akashic Records where the names and lifetimes of all souls are documented in an endless collection of books.

Doc notices a man whose attention is focused on a book that contains the lifetimes of Annie. He asks the man if he is the tracker and the man approaches their boat and confirms that he is. Turning to Chris the man asks him if *he* is the man who won't give up. Chris answers that he would go to hell and back to bring his Annie home. The tracker warns that it would not be hell's fury that would be a problem but more the possibility of losing one's sanity. Chris is undeterred, asking only when they would be leaving. The tracker tells him to close his eyes and think of Annie. When he does, their journey resumes.

As the boat exits the city to cross the ocean, the bright sunny day turns dark and flashes of lightning herald an approaching storm. The boat is tossed from side to side causing the men to grab whatever they can to keep from being knocked overboard. Chris points into the distance at what appears to be a school of fish moving towards the boat but when school arrives it is actually a group of tortured souls. The souls begin pushing the boat until it capsizes, knocking all three men into the sea. Under the water they are tossed around and quickly lose their sense of direction. Soon they wash up on the shores of hell.

Doc Albert is the first to get up. He moves toward the gates of hell, but as he approaches, the demons stand fast to keep them out. Chris can see the fear in Doc's eyes and he realizes that this is not really his fight; he needs to let Doc know that he has done enough. He tells his friend to go back; he will have to do this himself.

Chris and the tracker proceed further into Hell in search of Annie. The tracker tells Chris to keep focusing on Annie because that is the only way they will be able to find her. As Chris focuses his attention on finding Annie, a sea of faces appears and blocks their path. Hundreds of faces, the faces of the lost, call out to Chris and ask for his help. Then he sees Annie trapped in the center and he begins to run across the faces trying to reach her.

Suddenly the floor of faces breaks apart and he falls deep into the depths of hell. He lands in front of his and Annie's house; only the house now appears old and decrepit. He lies unconscious for a while until he is awakened by the voice of the tracker telling him that he must wake up, that time is running out. Chris has very little time to rescue Annie. There is also the possibility that Chris will lose his grip on reality and be trapped himself.

Chris enters the house and walks through the cobweb-infested rooms calling out for Annie. As he makes his way towards the master bedroom he hears her crying. She is sitting on the floor against their bed. Annie looks up at Chris and it's obvious that she does not recognize him. She tells him that she didn't always look the way she does. She tries to brush the cobwebs out of her hair. She looks around and remarks on the fact that the house seems to be falling apart. She explains that her husband Chris was the one to keep the house up. She wraps her arms around herself and shivers with the cold.

Chris pleads with her, trying to get her to recognize him and realize that *he* was the Chris she was talking about - he was her husband! Annie pulls away as he reaches out for her. She tells him that her husband Chris and her children are dead. Chris brings up every happy memory that he had with Annie, but she resists him in every way. Finally his thoughts begin to fade and it becomes more difficult to hold on to his own memories. He runs out of the house to find the tracker before he loses himself completely.

However, when the tracker consoles Chris by telling him that he had tried his best and had done all that he could have, Chris was having none of it. He decides that he is going to go back in and stay with Annie even if he loses his mind. He asks the tracker to go back to heaven and tell his children that he loves them.

Chris returns to Annie and as he lays his head in her lap he tells her that it looks like they were going to be in hell together. In the meantime, something has happened; there seems to have been a change. Chris's act of self-sacrifice has shifted the circumstances. While Chris begins to fade from consciousness, Annie starts to have flashes of memories from the good times with Chris and their children. Suddenly she recognizes Chris and cries out for him to come back to her. Sobbing, she begins to shake him.

The scene fades to white and shows Chris lying on a couch back in his own heaven. When he starts to come to, the thoughts of having failed Annie fill his heart. Then he hears Annie's voice - and there she is, right in his heaven along with both of their children! They promise to always be together in their heaven and when they reincarnate again back to earth. The final scene in the movie shows a young boy and girl who meet when their toy boats collide in a lake. We can safely assume that they are Chris and Annie in a future life.

What is the Concept of Hell?

Earlier I explained that the concept of heaven is thought, and our thoughts create our reality in heaven. That is why Chris's heaven was a replica of Annie's painting; that was something that filled his thoughts in life. On the other hand, Annie's life was filled with grief upon losing both her children and her husband and the despair that led to the taking of her own life. Her afterlife was influenced by her thoughts as well.

As a medium I find that those who have committed suicide are not trapped into eternal damnation but are in a place of healing. When a person's life is filled with misery and they are filled with negative thoughts, they will create a negative heaven for themselves for a time that we might perceive as a hell. The soul will spend some time playing out the life they lived and experience their death over and over until they come to terms about the way they had lived that life. In the astral realm there is no time, so the concept of eternity in hell is not accurate. Nor does the traditional picture of hell as a place of fire and brimstone run by a Satan with horns and carrying a pitchfork apply. Here is where I have to disagree about how hell is taught through the Christian religions.

Jesus Spoke on the Concept of Hell

When Jesus described the destiny of sinners who refused to change their ways, he compared it to Gehenna, which was a rubbish dump outside Jerusalem filled with people in wretched poverty who picked their way through it to find scraps. Huge fires which were burned to manage the trash lit up the night

Christian church leaders of mediaeval times took Jesus' description of the wretchedness in Gehenna literally. They preached of a judgment after death in which the wicked were thrown by devils into flames, while obedient churchgoers were lifted by angels into bliss.

Is there a Place called Hell?

The Old Testament does not mention a place called Hell at all. The word "Sheol" in the Old Testament is sometimes translated as Hell. By definition it is where everyone went when they died, good or evil, Jew or Gentile. The Jews did not believe in the concept of a Hell. It was never a place that the Jews were hoping to be saved from, since they didn't even believe in it! But they did need to be saved from their sins. Jesus came as the Anointed One to fulfill God's entire plan for the earth, that through Him might come salvation, deliverance of sin, peace, the kingdom of God, and all that God had promised through the Old Testament scriptures.

If Hell is real, why didn't God make that warning plain right at the beginning with Adam and Eve? God said the penalty for eating of the tree of Knowledge of Good and Evil was death - not eternal life in torment in fire and brimstone. Why didn't Moses warn about this fate in the Ten Commandments? Interestingly, the roots of hell are in paganism. Nations surrounding Israel believed in hell-like punishment in the afterlife, for they served bloodthirsty and evil gods. Why was the revelation of it first given to pagan nations, instead of the Israelites? Did God expect Israel to learn about the afterlife from the Pagan Gentiles? If so, why did He repeatedly warn Israel to not learn of their ways?

Is there a Satan?

The Hebrew word 'Satan' (שָׂטָן) translates to 'adversary' and comes from a Hebrew verb meaning 'to oppose' or 'to obstruct'. Satan is not a sentient being but a metaphor for the evil inclination - the 'yetzer hara' - that exists in every person and tempts us to do wrong. (In Judaism 'yetzer hara' refers to the inclination inherent in mortal man to do evil by violating the will of God.) The yetzer hara is not a force or a being, but rather refers to mankind's innate capacity for doing evil in the world.

Christian belief identifies Satan as Lucifer as well as the Devil; he is depicted as the supreme overlord of the hierarchy of Hell. To some, Satan is all-powerful while others limit his power to only corrupting or deceiving mankind. In some religions they do not regard Satan as pure evil but instead believe he was granted the ability to corrupt humanity in order to test faith.

I agree with what is written in the Old Testament about the concepts of hell and Satan. The evil in the world represents the negative consciousness that exists in the world today. As human beings we have the free will not to surrender to the evils of this world. I always preach that living by the Golden Rule, "Do unto others as you would have them do unto you" is the true secret of peace and happiness.

When we look at the concepts of Heaven and Earth, I feel that our life on earth is a version of Heaven and Hell. The earth is the schoolhouse of personal growth; by having all of the feelings of heaven and hell we have duality and choices in life to do right or wrong. When life seems bad and we are faced with depression and sadness and everything in our lives seems like it has gone wrong, we may feel life is like a living hell.

We most not give up, however, but we should choose instead to triumph over the challenges that arise in our lives. Eventually, as we persevere we are blessed in life by having peace, joy and happiness and our light shines so that we spread love around the world. We must embrace whatever comes our way; we have to have good and evil to help us learn what's wrong and right. So embrace the good in life and turn away from the temptation to give in to your inner 'yetzer hara'; that's the secret of having a life of fulfillment.

Dealing with Illness and Grief

Chapter Three

When a loved one develops a serious illness, it's normal to go through the emotional experience of grieving. If the illness is life threatening, it's important to talk about death and a plan for the end of life. These conversations can be difficult, but there are ways to make them easier. Time seems to freeze when we learn that someone we love has a life threatening illness. Sometime we stick our head in the sand hoping the news will go away or perhaps we will swing into action doing research on treatments and cures. Whatever action we take, we are trying to cope with a very challenging situation.

At some point, however, it may become clear that the end is drawing closer. That is when we need to reach out for emotional support for ourselves as we deal with the needs of the dying person. End of life care may need to be arranged and funeral plans be considered. Legal and financial matters must be addressed. We begin the anticipatory grieving process by dealing with issues when we begin grieving the loss of someone even before they die. Just as with grief after a death, family and friends may feel a multitude of different emotions that are typical at this time such as denial, sorrow, anxiety, anger, depression, and ultimately, acceptance. Although not everyone experiences anticipatory grief, such feelings are normal for those who do.

There are some steps that can help in dealing with the grief of losing someone. First, talking with someone who is sympathetic to the situation (especially if they have gone through the same ordeal) can be helpful. Additionally there are many types of support groups for people who are going through loss. Also be aware that our emotions may have an impact on the person who is dying. Sometimes dying people hold on to life because they sense that others aren't ready to let them go. We should reassure them that it is okay for them to let go and let them know that those left behind will be okay. Although painful in so many ways, a terminal illness also offers time to express our love, to share our appreciation, and to make amends when necessary. Make the time to say goodbye properly; it is very important. In so many readings I have done where death had occurred unexpectedly, people who have lost loved ones often regret not having had a chance to say goodbye or having spent more time with their loved one before their passing.

How to Talk About Death

Talking honestly about death is often difficult because we may fear that it will seem as though we are abandoning our loved one and giving up on them. In my readings I find that some people that are near death are comforted by the thought that they will be embraced rather than abandoned no matter what happens. Some are afraid and want empathy.

They may be stifling their own fears and anxieties about leaving their loved ones, losing control, becoming a burden, and leaving tasks and plans unfinished. Many people fear a painful death or being alone., not everyone who is terminally ill is ready to talk about death but for those who are, the comfort and release they will gain from open and honest dialog about their situation is profound.

To start this difficult conversation it is best to look for openings. For example, you could talk about a book you read on the topic or discuss someone else's illness and death that unfolded in the same way. You can ask questions such as "Is there anything you want to talk about?" These questions may help to ease into the conversation about death. Depending on your loved one's comfort level and receptiveness to these topics, you might even share your thoughts about the afterlife. If a conversation feels too difficult for either the dying person or the caregiver, end it or let them end it. In that case it might be better to allow him or her to hold on to comforting thoughts and wishful thinking of the possibility of getting better.

If you find that you have trouble starting a conversation about death, get help from the experts. Seek spiritual counsel. Talk with your religious leader or counselor. Priests, rabbis, and other religious leaders can offer real comfort to those who are believers. Even people who do not regularly attend religious services may turn toward their faith as an illness progresses. A doctor's reassurance about how physical symptoms might unfold and how pain will be handled can also be invaluable.

Hospice workers and hospital social workers can also help you and the person who is ill as you both grapple with the issues surrounding death. The hospice team works with the patient to develop a personal plan of care. Family members, partners, and close friends may be invited to help in many ways such as by assisting with daily tasks like feeding and bathing and offering comfort through reading, sharing music, holding hands, or simply being present. Hospice staff can administer pain medications, provide nursing care, and offer emotional support. Before and after a death, emotional support is extended to caregivers as well. Many programs offer bereavement counseling after a death. The hospice team typically includes specially trained doctors, nurses, aides, social workers, counselors, therapists, people who offer spiritual care, and volunteers.

(Source: Hospice Foundation of America)

Understanding the Grieving Process

Losing someone you love deeply is very painful. We may experience all kinds of difficult emotions and it may feel like the pain and sadness that we are experiencing will never go away. These are normal reactions in the grieving process. Is there a right or wrong way to grieve? The answer is no, but there are healthy ways to cope with the pain. Grief is a natural response to loss; it is the emotional suffering we feel when someone we love passes away. The more significant the loss, the more intense the grief will be.

The grieving process takes time and the healing will gradually happen. This is a process and it cannot be forced or hurried. There is no timetable for grieving; it is up to the individual as to the amount of time it will take. The most important thing to do is to be patient with ourselves and allow the process to unfold naturally no matter how long it takes.

Everyone grieves differently; it all depends on our personality as to how we cope with loss. Ignoring our pain or keeping it pent up inside will only make it worse. It is necessary to face grief in order for the healing to begin. Feelings of sadness and loneliness are normal when we lose someone. Some people may think crying is a sign of weakness but it is not; it is a way of releasing our emotions. We don't need to put on a brave face for our family and friends. Showing them our true feelings will actually help them heal as well. Sometimes there are people who just can't cry, but if they don't express themselves through crying, they may simply have other ways of showing it. There is no right or wrong time frame for grieving. How long it takes may differ from person to person and may come in stages. The classic stages of grief include: Stage One – Anger, Stage Two – Bargaining, Stage Three – Denial, Stage Four – Depression, and Stage Five – Acceptance.

If you are experiencing any of these emotions after the loss of a loved one, it may help to know that your reaction is natural and that you'll heal in time. The order of stages may vary for different people except for the last stage of acceptance. The stages are guidelines for what to expect during the grieving period, but not everyone has to go through all of these stages in order to heal from grieving. Some people may resolve their grief without going through any of the stages, it is up to the person in the way they process their grief. Grieving is a process. It has its ups and downs and its highs and lows. It is rough at the beginning and becomes less intense as time goes by. Reminders throughout the years will be triggers that will bring on a fresh wave of grief; these can include special events like family weddings, birthdays, and even other funerals.

Initially you may experience shock and disbelief, feel numb, and have trouble focusing. You may also experience a sense of unreality like you are losing your mind, or have thoughts that it was all a bad dream. At times you will be expecting the person you lost to walk into the room at any given moment even though you know they are gone. Often people will question their own religious beliefs after the loss of a loved one.

Some will feel profound sadness with feelings of emptiness, despair and loneliness, emotional instability, and bouts of crying. There may be regrets or feelings of guilt about things you might have done differently or things that you didn't say or do. Some will feel guilty at the sense of relief that can come after the person has died from a long, draining illness, or for not having prevented the death even when there was nothing in their power that they could have actually done. Even if the death was no one's fault, you may feel angry and be resentful over the situation or even for some reason you may be angry with yourself.

Being angry sometime will lead to blaming doctors, God, or others for the injustice that was done. After a significant loss you may feel anxious and helpless, causing panic attacks to arise as the thought of facing life alone without that person starts to become a reality. We often think of grief as a strictly emotional process, but grief can involve physical problems as well, including fatigue, nausea ,weight loss or weight gain, aches and pains, and insomnia.

Support in the Grieving Process

The most important factor in healing from a loss is having the support of other people. Sharing your burden of grief will make it easier for you to cope. Even if you aren't comfortable talking about your feelings, it is so important to express them when you're grieving. Do not grieve alone; turn to family and friends and lean on those who care about you the most. Whenever support comes your way, accept it with gratitude rather than avoiding the help. Let people know what you need. Oftentimes people want to help but don't know how, so it's important to tell them what you need.

I find that spiritual activities like meditating; praying, or going to mourning rituals can provide a sense of peace. If you have a religious tradition, embrace it. Join a bereavement support group in your area as well. If your grief is too overwhelming, talk with a grief counselor. They can help you work through the intense emotions and obstacles that you need to overcome through the grieving process. Eventually you may be ready to consult a medium. People have commented that the work I do as a medium gave them far more closure then having counseling sessions, so find a reputable medium and get the closure you are seeking.

Taking Care of Yourself

It is important to take care of yourself during the grieving process. The stress of a major loss can quickly deplete your emotional reserves. Looking after your physical and emotional needs will help you get through this difficult time. You must face your feelings and not suppress them in order to heal.

By acknowledging the feelings you have, you will heal at a faster pace then by suppressing the sadness. Unresolved grief can lead to complications such as long-term depression, anxiety, substance abuse, and health problems. When you are feeling good physically you will also feel better mentally.

It's important to get enough sleep, eat a good diet, and get some exercise. Stay away from alcohol or drugs that will numb the pain; you are only masking your grief and not working through it. Writing a journal about things you want to express to a loved one or making a scrapbook celebrating their life will help in the grieving process. Also I find that creating a memorial page on Facebook is a great way of honoring your loved ones; it also helps with the grieving process for yourself and for other friends and family members. You can also find an organization or cause that was important to your loved one and get involved.

By the same token, it's okay to be angry, yell to the heavens, or just cry it out. No one can tell you when it's time or not time to grieve or how to feel. If you feel like laughing, do so; laughter always is a great way to take away depression. Plan ahead for anniversaries, birthdays, holidays, and special occasions that can trigger grief. If you're sharing an event that will trigger grief with other relatives or friends, talk to them ahead of time and agree on strategies to honor the person you loved. You *will* get through this difficult time in your life.

Time Heals but the Pain Never Goes Away

As time passes, the emotions should become less intense as you accept the loss and start to move forward. If you aren't feeling better over time or your grief is getting worse, it may be a sign that your grief has developed into a more serious problem such as complicated grief or major depression. Unfortunately, the pain of losing someone you loved dearly never goes away but it should become bearable in time. If it doesn't - if your loss has become the complete focus of your life - you are experiencing complicated grief. Complicated grief is being stuck in an intense state of mourning for an extended period of time. You may have trouble accepting the death long after it has occurred. It disrupts your daily routine and undermines everyone and everything in your life. Some signs of complicated grief include an intense longing for the deceased love one, denial of the death of the loved one, or a feeling that life is empty or meaningless.

The Difference Between Grief and Depression

Grief and clinical depression share many symptoms but there are ways to tell the difference between the two. Grief has mixed emotions. There will be ups and downs and highs and lows; it is never a consistent emotion. With depression, on the other hand, the feelings of emptiness and despair are constant. You may have an intense feeling of guilt, thoughts of suicide, or feelings of hopelessness or worthlessness. If you recognize any of the symptoms of complicated grief or clinical depression, talk to a mental health professional right away. Also get help if you are blaming yourself for their death or for failing to prevent it or if you are having difficulty staying focused and you feel disconnected from others.

Transitions Into The Afterlife

Chapter Four

Throughout time humanity has seen death as something dreadful. In most cultures people try to avoid or minimize the concept of death. The fear of death, however, is actually the fear of the unknown and by learning the true nature of death we can be released from the bondage of that fear. If people only knew for certain what really happens when we die, there wouldn't be so much fear surrounding this topic.

After a person dies, the journey of their soul truly becomes a great adventure in which the soul transitions from one realm of life into another. What the soul experiences varies from person to person because of the circumstances revolving around each unique life path and the specifics of each death. It can be an amazing experience for those who have crossed over according to their life plan. It can be a confusing experience for those who have passed away unexpectedly. It can be a painful experience for those who committed suicide as well as for those who have become lost souls whose death was a horrific experience through war, murder, or tyranny.

In my line of work I get to hear many stories from the other side describing the experience of death and I have found that souls experience death at many levels. Death is not an end, but a rebirth. This means that the soul is returning to its natural form of being Godlike as an energetic light-body of unconditional love. I frequently correct people when they refer to me as one who speaks to the dead. I like to point out that in reality I'm talking with the living in a different form because the soul is made in God's image and it is everlasting.

Death by Illness

We all have free will to choose a particular path according to our soul plan when in human form. At times we find that our path is so full of difficulties and adversaries that we wonder what we might have done to deserve such a life. The truth is that you plan your life and the challenges that you will face before you are even born. When you were still in the astral realm as an energetic being you planned the details of how your life would be from your birth until your death. This is known as your "Soul Agenda" or "Life Plan". These are binding energetic commitments, agreements or contracts which involve not just ourselves as single human beings but our over-soul (the God-like aspect of ourselves) and many others from our soul family with whom we will have future interaction as parents, partners, children, and friends.

The final part of a soul agreement has to do with the way we transition from this earth. Death is something we can't run from; it will happen sooner or later. Death is a learning experience and will come to the soul according to its life plan. It doesn't matter how old the person is nor does the cause of death matter. The time and circumstances of each death vary as much as the souls who create them. That is why there are early deaths in life, unexpected accidents, and death from sickness as well as death in old age through natural causes.

I'm often asked why someone's loved one died of a serious illness. I tell people it is because that person had agreed to it in advance as their soul plan for their own growth. Many people have a hard time believing this because it is a strongly held societal belief that illness is something that happens to us and that it's outside of our control or it occurs only through the lack of taking care of ourselves. The rather startling truth is, however, that you direct your illness according to your soul plan.

We are here on Earth to grow and to learn lessons and one avenue for such growth is to choose to accept the experiences of illness. This doesn't mean that all illness leads to death. Your soul plan might be that you will do everything in your power to get better and you survive the illness. It's a hard concept to grasp but in reality the events surrounding an illness and death affect not only the loved one who dies of the illness but also the people who are a part of their soul plan. For example, imagine parents who lose a child to a major disease being inspired by the loss of their child to raise awareness about the disease and causing funding to become available towards finding a cure. This is one way that a life plan can work; the death of a loved one will have a ripple effect that will sometimes inspire others do their part according to the family soul plan.

Another soul may need to learn a lesson about loss and how to focus on what is important in life. Think of a person who is strongly dependent on others. Part of their life plan may be learning how to be stronger on their own after losing someone on whom they always depended.

What Happens After Death?

Most people know me as a Spiritual Healing Medium, but I am also an Ordained Minister. Occasionally I'm asked to put on my minister hat to officiate a church service or pay my respects to a person in hospice care. One day I received a phone call from a daughter whose mother was in hospice. Joan, her mother, had cancer that was in its final stages. She told me that her mother was afraid of death and because she had read my book ***"Is There More to Life Than What We Know?"*** she wanted more answers about the afterlife, so I went to visit her.

Joan asked that I sit next to her on the bed so she would be able to hold my hand as she told me her life story. "Joseph, I've had cancer since I was a young woman. It started as breast cancer and now it has spread all over my body. My eightieth birthday is today and I feel that I have had a blessed life. I have three children and five grandchildren but I very much miss my husband who passed away ten years ago. Will I see him in Heaven? But also…I am so afraid to close my eyes and never wake up!"

I told Joan the concept of heaven that I have outlined in previous chapters and assured her that her husband would be first in line to greet her. Then she asked me why she had cancer most of her adult life. I decided not to confuse her at this stage by trying to explain that we choose to be sick according to our life plan, but I wanted her to appreciate some of the sense of growth her experience had given her. "Joan, your sickness made you the strong person that you are today. You have shown your family that no matter how bad it gets you can stay tough and fight through." She loved the answers I gave to her, squeezing my hand and thanking me as she laid her head back on her pillow with a smile on her face.

As her daughter escorted me out of the room she told me that she'd had a private reading with me around five years before. In her reading her maternal grandparents had came through as well as her mother's sister. She told me that the best part of the reading had been when her father had come through telling her that he would always be by her mother's side and he would be the first to greet her when she passed. Then she had asked me about her mother's health. I had asked her how old her mother was, which at the time was seventy-four and I had told her that within four or five years she would become very sick and might not even make it to her eightieth birthday. As it turned out, Joan passed away two days after her eightieth birthday. I hope that I was able to give her a vision of heaven that helped to ease her passing.

Death by Accidents

While some people will have a lingering death through an illness with time to put their affairs in order and to say good-bye, sudden deaths by accident such as a car accident, a drowning, or an accidental overdose are a different story. In my line of work I have received many questions asking if the accident could have been prevented. It all depends on what your soul intended. In our life plan, if we are meant to die in an accident it will happen according to the plan.

If you survive a near-fatal accident, it is because a guardian angel stepped in to keep you from harm's way and to keep you on your intended path. For those who are injured in an accident, the therapy and recovery are part of their life plan lesson. When a person is suddenly stricken down by an accident, they had agreed to die that way according to their life plan to help those who are left here on earth as they pursue their own earthly goals.

This could be family members or even total strangers; it can be anyone who was affected by the death. We are all connected! There is a reason for each death at that given time and in the manner in which each soul passes. If the dying person had been an organ donor, their organ parts help other individuals continue on in life and that person being helped was a part of their soul agenda. They might teach a lesson about dying with dignity to those left behind or in other cases they might inspire those left behind to love and treasure one another as we know not the hour nor the day

Those who cross over from sudden accidental death are surprised to find themselves on the other side, but after receiving guidance and comfort from loving spiritual guides they begin to understand what has happened and to accept the fact of their death. During this time the soul is drawn to the light and will have a longing to reunite with its oversoul. On some subconscious level the soul knows that this is going to happen and begins to sense the presence of loved ones who have already crossed over. As part of the life plan the soul will have pre-programmed who the loved ones will be that will be waiting to meet them at the time of impact and instant death. The soul reconnects with it soul family and becomes omnipresent, meaning it can be everywhere at once visiting their loved ones who are left behind.

Sometimes souls cross over in groups. One of the most memorable incidents of multiple crossings, the terrorist attacks of September 11, 2001, on the twin towers in New York City serve as a powerful example. Thousands of souls crossed over that day. Most would have first felt a sense of confusion as to what had happened that would then have created a whirlwind of activities on both sides, here on the earth as well as on the spiritual side. If we were able to see beyond the veil we would have witnessed thousands of souls being greeted by many spiritual guides, loved ones and angels to help them make their transition. There is also a great deal of love and connection within such a mass group of souls. Because they all perished together there would have been understanding and acceptance of the souls to remain together as the group transitioned together. Once this had taken place each individual spirit would soon finds its own connection with its loved ones and would begin its own individual spirit journey.

Since there is no time in the astral realm, there is no telling how long the transition would have taken. It all depends on the individual. Some might at first be in denial, trying to re-attach themselves to their physical body and refusing guidance from their spiritual counselors. Others might be more open to the communication from their guides and family members in spirit and willing to allow themselves to be led forward; they would quickly lose the feeling that they were alone. Regardless of their religious background, the sight of their loved one on the other side is a key to success for the soul to transition from its earthly life.

Forgiveness

There is additional emotion to deal with for those who have died of sudden death caused by another individual, such as a car accident caused by another driver who was in some way at fault. As with other sudden deaths, the individual will not be prepared for it and will often cross over in a state of confusion, but the anger must also be dealt with. Loved ones and spiritual guides will gather to help welcome them but also to counsel them as this particular type of crossing over can be at times a little more difficult for the newly deceased. Their spiritual counselors as well as their loved ones help to cushion the impact and explain the sudden changes they are feeling and how to move through the anger to forgiveness. It is also important for those of us who are left behind to forgive the person who caused the accidental death of our loved one. By forgiving them we release the negative energies of anger and hate that can bring our own vibration down and we can begin to heal, as does the one who has crossed over

Instead of remaining embroiled in anger and bitterness, we must embrace forgiveness. Forgiveness can lead to a higher vibration of peace, joy, and happiness. Releasing your anger will free your soul to live life with a sense of closure. Remember, forgiving doesn't mean forgetting. Once we experience loss we are never the same. The memory will always be in our mind consciously and subconsciously but ultimately, it's how we choose to deal with our emotions that are key to our soul's growth.

At first, negative thoughts and feelings actually feel comforting and reassuring because they are familiar so it becomes difficult to break free from them. I have observed that many people refuse to forgive because they need someone to blame for all of the pain and suffering they experience when losing someone, but in fact through the act of forgiving we are releasing all of our anger and sadness. It is not easy to let go of the past and all the pain but if you can manage to rise above the lower vibration and forgive, it will make you stronger than ever. It will also allow you to accomplish one of your life-lesson goals of learning lessons about forgiveness.

Accidental Deaths

As a medium I frequently connect with souls who have died from accidents. Most are vehicle-related, with motorcycle accidents topping the list. Boating accidents are also common in south Florida where I live. There was one reading that really hit me hard when I read for parents who had lost their son through a boating accident. Children who die from accidents generally know on some level that this is what is going to happen to them and that their life span on earth will be short. It has to do with not only their own life lessons but oftentimes with how they can help all of the people who are a part of their soul agenda.

During the reading I felt a very young presence and asked the couple if they had lost a young son. They confirmed that their son Jason had been eight when he died. Then I felt a tightness in my lungs as if they were filling with water and asked if their son drowned. They told me that yes; he had died in a boating accident. I looked at the father and asked, "Have you forgiven the person who was responsible for taking your boy's life? Your son was very close to this man and has forgiven him as well; he says it was an accident." The father answered, "It was my brother who was driving the boat. The boat hit a wave that caused my son to hit his head, and he was thrown into the ocean. Within seconds our son was lost to us. The nightmare of his death replays over and over in our minds. It's not my brother's fault, so there is no need to forgive him. I can see his pain every time we are together."

Jason had more messages for his family. "Your son is telling me that he loves his family. He says that you and your brother coached his football team and you both fought over who was the head coach when the team won; he is laughing now as he tells me this." Next was a message for Jason's mother - "I love the stuffed bears that you're selling to raise money for a children's foundation in my honor." He also told his mom to give his older brother the message that he loves him and that he had been the best brother any boy could have. Another reading was a 'Born to Wild' reading when the spirit of the boyfriend of a woman in my audience came riding in on his Harley motorcycle. He flashed his tattooed arm towards me with the name 'Lucy', which happened to be his girlfriend's name. It was supposed to be a short cigarette run to the store around the corner but a car swerved into him as he was passing the car. Next he told me, *"We were supposed to go on vacation that week and I had finally worked up the nerve; I was planning to ask Lucy to marry me on the cruise to Mexico!"* I relayed this information to Lucy and with tears in her eyes she confirmed everything.

Then I felt him merge with me and he had me get on one knee. I asked for her hand, opened her palm, and with my index finger I began to draw a heart on the palm of her hand. “It's not me, it’s your boyfriend and he wants me to ask you to marry him.” By now she was crying uncontrollably as she explained that he used to draw hearts on her body; this absolutely had to be him. I drew her up from her chair and explained that he would like to hug her and as he and I gave her a hug together, I (he) again asked, “Will you marry me?” There wasn’t a dry eye in the house as she answered, “Yes!”

Illness and Death of Infants

We will begin by talking about the soul of a baby in the planning stages for its soul agenda. This is when the soul is researching parents to whom they wish to be born when they reincarnate. The soul will look for an environment that will best help to evolve them in their spiritual journey. Once a soul has chosen a family and has a general overview of their life plans according to their soul agenda, they are born, erasing all memory of past incarnations.

But what happens with stillborn deaths or sudden infant deaths? When a baby who has not been delivered yet returns to heaven, they do not go through the death process of reviewing their life because they are still connected to heaven and have not made any earthly attachments.

They still have the knowledge of the oversoul and their soul family and return immediately to their full spirit incarnation. They are greeted by their soul family and by spiritual counselors who help them understand what has happened to them and why they returned back to heaven so quickly. When the baby's soul comes back into its true mature spirit form, because it hasn't lost its connection to heaven and it maintains all of its past life memories, it is immediately aware of its soul agenda.

Children will interact with their earthly family from the other side after their death. It is a time of deep sorrow for the loved ones who are still reeling at the death of their child. The young soul will try to help their loved ones overcome such an experience for a period of time, but eventually it must move on and let their loved ones work through their grief and sorrow. There was a reason for that child to be on this earth and a reason for it to leave so soon. It is not always for us to know why, but as a medium I'm able to help the parents to understand why the child was a part of their life, and how in heaven they are playing a part that is greater then we can imagine.

Miscarriages

During the time that a baby is carried in the mother's womb, there are many things that can happen to cause a miscarriage. In most cases the fetus is not maturing or might not be healthy enough to go full term and the soul will abort itself to try again in the future when the fetus is healthy. As human beings we are born with free will and because of that we can change our soul agenda at any given time.

The baby's soul has free will, too, and may feel that it made a mistake. It may decide, for example, that it has not chosen the right set of parents to complete its soul agenda and will decide to back out, leading to a miscarriage. It may also happen when the parents are having problems in their life or the mother is going through stress or resentment about having the child. Another reason is that some souls are so eager to come back to reincarnate right after death that they don't take the time to fully make their transition. They find themselves reincarnating too soon and when they recognize this fact they may also end the pregnancy.

Sudden Infant Death Syndrome

As in the case of miscarriage, infants who die from sudden infant death syndrome are often souls who feel that the timing was not right to incarnate. Once they get to earth they feel that they have made a mistake. There can be many reasons that the soul decides not to continue with the incarnation to fulfill their soul agenda with the parents they have chosen but are given an opportunity to die from such conditions as SIDS. Oftentimes baby souls will agree to reincarnate for a very short time knowing that their purpose was to help the spiritual evolution of all involved (including itself) through the experience of the birth and death.

Abortion

Through my work as a medium I do bring through a lot of souls whose mothers aborted them. Usually the mother is left feeling guilty for having taken the baby's life. One question that I'm asked is whether or not a baby has a soul when it's in its mother's womb. The answer is yes and no.

When the fetus is in the womb, the soul will continually enter and exit the fetus, not quite making its new body home. The moment when the baby takes its first breath is when the soul enters completely and is committed to stay within the human body and fulfill its soul agenda. If the mother has an abortion for whatever reason, the soul will return to its soul family until it has another opportunity to reincarnate.

The mother has free will to choose abortion. The baby soul has no control over the mother's free will, but the mother must understand that there is a ripple effect when terminating a pregnancy. The baby soul had chosen the mother for a reason according to their soul agenda and now this agenda cannot be fulfilled. Then there are times when the baby soul will agree to the abortion knowing beforehand that it will play a big part in the evolution of both its mother and itself in terms of learning spiritual lessons. Abortion is not considered a spiritual crime because of free will.

Childhood Diseases and Deformities

Infants who at the time of birth are born with physical problems have agreed to accept this assignment for many reasons. When a baby is born with some kind of mental or physical deformity, the soul of that infant has chosen to go through these experiences because they need to experience the challenges as part of their soul agenda. Children who endure long-term illnesses have agreed to this before they incarnate and are aware of what they are going to be experiencing before they are born. They write the details into their soul plan to promote their own spiritual growth.

Death by Suicide

Some religions teach that suicide is an unforgivable sin. There can be no doubt that the act of killing oneself is a sin in light of the sixth commandment where God says, "You shall not murder" (Exodus 20:13) and suicide is murdering oneself. I feel that the sixth commandment was written to protect other souls and does not necessarily pertain to our own soul since it is ours to do with as we wish. We should not be so quick to condemn a person who dies by their own hand because it is their own free will that allowed them to choose to leave this earth.

Would God condemn someone for all eternity? The answer is no, God does not pass judgment because God is all forgiving and aware of the limitation of the human soul and its lack of a full understanding of God's Laws. Suicide is shocking and has a traumatic effect upon those who survive, but it is not a 'worse sin' than others. We humans are the ones who judge. The typical assumption that many bible-believing people make about the afterlife is that there are only two possible options: that one either goes directly to heaven or straight to hell upon dying. In fact nowhere does the bible teach that heaven is the reward of the saved or that everyone else is condemned to eternal condemnation and hellfire.

Coping With Suicidal Thoughts

Before we consider the implications of suicide in the afterlife, I would first like to focus on dealing with suicide in general. Some common situations or life events that might cause suicidal thoughts include grief, sexual abuse, financial problems, remorse, rejection, relationship breakup, and unemployment. No matter what the cause, suicidal thoughts are the result of feeling like you can't cope when you're faced with what seems to be an overwhelming life situation. There also may be a genetic link to suicide. People who are victims of suicide or who have suicidal thoughts or behavior are more likely to have a family history of suicide.

When feelings of hopelessness, isolation, and despair become too heavy to bear, you might feel so overwhelmed with pain that suicide seems like the only way to release yourself from the burden you've been carrying. Anyone who reaches this state should know that there is help available to deal with suicidal feelings. Contacting a mental health professional can help people heal and experience joy and happiness again no matter how impossible that may seem. Here is a list of suicide prevention measures for anyone who is in crisis that I found by searching the web.

Preventing Suicide *(Suicide Prevention Research)*

1. Put off any plans. Promise yourself that you'll wait 48 hours before doing anything. Remember, thoughts don't have the power to force you to act. Sometimes extreme pain can distort our perception. Waiting before taking action will give your mind time to clear.

2. Seek professional help immediately. Suicidal thoughts can feel overwhelming, and there's no reason to fight them alone. Ask a professional for help by calling emergency services or contacting a suicide hotline. These services have trained people ready to listen to you and offer help 24/7. Suicidal thoughts and impulses are very serious.

3. Go to the hospital. If you have called for help and are still experiencing suicidal thoughts, you need to go to the emergency room. Ask someone you trust to drive you, or call emergency services. In the United States, it's illegal for emergency rooms to turn you away in an emergency, even if you don't have health insurance or can't pay.

4. Call a trusted friend or loved one. Your risk of suicide is increased if you're alone with suicidal thoughts. Don't bottle them up or keep them to yourself. Call someone you love and trust and share your thoughts with him or her. Sometimes just talking to a good listener can help you cope and be enough to calm your thoughts. Stay on the phone, or ask the person to come over and be with you so you're not on your own.

You may feel worried or embarrassed about talking to someone about your feelings. The people who love you will not judge you for sharing these feelings with them. They will be glad that you called rather than trying to handle everything on your own. You can't predict when new options might appear. It's impossible to know what might happen if you just wait a few more days. If you act on your thoughts now, you'll never find out what could have been.

5. Wait for help. If you've called emergency services or a friend to come over, focus on keeping yourself safe while you're on your own. Take deep, calming breaths and repeat some coping statements to yourself. You could even write these statements down to reinforce them in your mind: *My depression is talking, not me...I will get through this...I'm just having thoughts right now - they can't make me do anything...There are other ways to handle my feelings.*

6. Stop using drugs and alcohol. You might be trying to make the thoughts go away by drinking or using drugs, but adding these chemicals to your body actually just makes it a lot harder to think clearly, which you need to be able to do to cope with suicidal thoughts. If you're drinking or doing any drugs right now, stop and give your mind a break. Many people may use alcohol and other narcotics as antidepressants, but the relief that they provide is merely transitory.

If you don't feel like you can stop, be with someone else - don't stay by yourself. Avoid being alone. Solitude does not help suicidal thoughts; in fact, it can worsen them to a great extent.

Spiritual Perspective of Suicide

Let's talk about suicide and its aftereffects from a spiritual perspective. It all begins with your life plan when you pick your parents and life circumstances. A life plan is like a script for a play; you are accepting a role in the play of life. So you incarnated and you're playing your role in life until one day your role seems to be getting harder to perform. You may be dealing with depression or addictions. Your life and dreams come crashing down around you. For whatever reason, the role you're in just doesn't make you happy any longer and you want to quit your role by committing suicide.

Now your life plan has changed all future circumstances and the people in your life have to change their own life path plan in order to deal with not having you as an actor in the play as well as experience the grief and the guilt of not being able to stop you from committing suicide. What happens next? You're responsible for leaving them in a mess and you are held responsible for fixing it from the other side.

When you commit suicide, you're not just leaving a role; you are changing the outcome of the play, which can affect countless people's lives by altering their own life plan. Think if you were meant to give your parents grandchildren. Now the play has changed; not only will they not have grandchildren but if you were an only child, they are now childless. If you had siblings, their lives will be strongly impacted as well. Having free will gives you an out in giving up your role, but you cannot give up the responsibility you had in that role.

I find that most suicides have deep sorrow and regret for having ended their life on earth. They find themselves feeling ashamed and guilty for hurting the ones they love. They want to do everything in their power to help the people they left behind. When communicating with souls who have committed suicide, I have learned that the soul feels it is trapped in a place that Catholics would describe as Purgatory. In truth, it is called 'the place of learning'. People who end up in this place should not judge themselves too harshly, because God does not judge.

He is all forgiving. In this place souls will go over their life plan and see where it all came undone. They will relive their death and witness the grief that they have brought upon others until the lesson is learned. These souls will not be alone; crossed-over loved ones, spirit guides, or angels will help them get through the pain that they caused others. Many religions preach that suicides will be stuck in such a hellish state for eternity, but this is not true. In my work I help suicides cross over all of the time. When they reach the heavenly state of mind, the soul is healed and surrounded with unconditional love and forgiveness.

So, you are allowed to quit your life plan and free will ensures that you have the right to take your own life. But you must be aware of the consequences and the responsibility you have to every single person whose life you would have touched in a significant way. Life for everyone can be complicated and hard. The earth is the hardest place to live and you have chosen your life here in order to learn from the lessons that life on earth has in store. When you quit you still have to learn all the lessons you came here to learn, so the next time you incarnate it isn't going to get easier; in fact, it will probably be harder. Life is a performance and we are actors in the play of life. If we act out the play in its entirety, then we don't have to come back again to redo the same play all over again.

Murder and Mass Murders

Souls of people who have been murdered are instantly in a state of shock. There will be spirit guides and angels to help comfort them and to help them understand what has happened. After this initial period of shock has worn off they will begin to see loved ones who have crossed over before them. Seeing their loved ones will offer comfort as the soul begins to realize what has taken place. Because the soul was suddenly taken from their life, their emotions are still somewhat intact and that allows them to have feelings of anger and sadness. It's a feeling that they usually don't hold for long but it's there to help them with closure in making their transition.

There are sometimes victims of murder in spirit who cannot move past their emotions and will cling to the earth not making the transition towards their oversoul. No matter how much the spirit guides, angels, and loved ones try to help them cross over, they are unwilling to do so. These are the souls that are known as Lost Souls.The soul has free will and if it chooses not to make its transition into the heavenly realm, then it will stay earth-bound with the emotions of anger, sadness and resentment towards the person that caused their death. In my work as a medium I have helped many souls that are stuck in this limbo to move past this and on into the heavenly realm.

Honors to Officer William Myers

William "Bill" James Myers, age 64, of Shalimar, Florida, passed away in the line of duty on Sept. 22, 2015. Bill served his country in the United States Air Force for over 20 years as an Air Traffic Controller; and he was a proud member of the Okaloosa County Sheriff's Department for over 20 years. Sheriff's deputy Bill Myers died following an early Tuesday morning shooting in Shalimar. According to the sheriff's office, retired deputy Bill Myers returned to the force in January to work part-time helping serve court documents. He initially retired in November 2013 after serving almost 25 years with the agency.

I was invited to a store call "Stone Soup" in Fort Walton Beach, Florida, to facilitate a weekend of events. The shop owner, Jan Myers, was very excited to have me and told me she had a full house for all of the events. During my "Speaking to Heaven" gallery, Jan was in the back of the audience taking pictures when a spirit named Bill came into the room. No one in the audience seemed to be able to identify him until I mentioned that he had been a police officer; as it turned out it was Jan's husband who had been killed in the line of duty.

I felt Bill's personality strongly as he told Jan to 'plant her butt in a chair'. Bill talked about his funeral processional and how the whole town had come out to pay their respects. He told Jan that he had seen her on his motorcycle as she rode on the back of it with a friend during the processional. He went on to tell her about how he was in a good place and loved her very much. My feeling is that Bill made his transition and is not holding on to the anger that could keep him earthbound and that he is looking after Jan, hoping that she will heal and forgive the person who ended his life.

Ghost & Lost Souls

What Are Ghosts?

Ghosts are the spirits of dead people that for various reasons are stuck between this plane of existence and the next, usually as a result of some tragedy or trauma. The Hollywood versions of ghosts and hauntings almost always depict them as scary and threatening, but that is not generally the case. Ghosts are indeed trapped in our earthly world; they are wandering spirits who are struggling in a temporary hell, unable to move beyond their past. But most of them have more in common with your befuddled great-aunt who gets lost at Wal-Mart than they do with the malevolent manifestation of the Amityville Horror.

Ghosts are frequently unaware of their true physical surroundings and often when they appear they will project the surroundings of their own time in history. Some ghosts are not even the soul of a person but actually a glimpse of a past event that has energetically imprinted in that place and time that replays within the physical environment.

What is a Lost Soul?

Lost souls are spiritually adrift for whatever reason. They block the intuitive guidance from their spiritual guides that could help them at their time of their transition. By doing this they also cut themselves off from experiencing the unconditional love of their soul family. Rather than quickly moving into peace and serenity in the afterlife, they experience a period of struggle and may feel angry or sad.

The movie *"Ghost"* comes to mind as a great example of a lost soul. When Sam (Patrick Swayze) was murdered, he refused to go into the light but chose instead to find out who killed him. He closed himself off from his spiritual counselors and instead found a medium named Oda Mae (Whoopi Goldberg) to help him find justice. After he accomplished his mission of justice he was able to hear the voices of his spiritual counselors as the white light appeared to him.

Lost souls are operating from their ego, not from their higher self. Because they are ego-driven, lost souls will often feel the need to defend their position and assert that they are right and that they know best. There are many reasons why souls choose to stay in our physical realm instead of crossing over. If they have passed suddenly, have unfinished business, or they were especially mired in heavy emotions at the time of their death, or even if there were unresolved issues surrounding the growth of their soul, they may choose to linger. However, it is always the individual's choice. We have incarnated in a lifetime of free will and experience. If you ever feel the presence of these spirits and wish to help them transition into the Light and continue on their soul's journey, here are some things that you can do.

Crossing Over a Lost Soul

Start with a prayer to set your intentions and ask for protection and for God's help in transitioning the lost soul into the heavenly realm. It is important to talk to the lost soul with compassion; remember, they were once a living person just like you before they died. There is no need to yell or shout like in the movies. If you do, the soul might actually feel very scared and confused.

Consider that the soul is not intentionally frightening or haunting you. What you may be picking up on is the soul's own fears and confusion about crossing over. This is actually very common so remember to have compassion when communicating. Introduce yourself and reassure the spirit that it is going to be fine.

It's best to talk with the lost soul out loud. If you are able to hear them it will be telepathically, or you may just feel their emotions. They could also appear as a shadow, color patterns, or be translucent. The temperature of the room may change as well. Since there are no such things as time and space in the astral realm, the lost soul can be "trapped" for hundreds or even thousands of years without realizing how much time has gone by (or that any time has actually passed) since their death. Sometimes, the lost soul only needs to know the year and be assured that their loved ones are waiting for them on the other side.

You may also need to remind them that it is safe for them to cross and nothing bad will happen to them. At times the lost soul may not be trapped but may just be afraid to cross over and so they wait for someone like you to help them cross when they feel ready. Helping a lost soul transition can be a very powerful experience; it is an experience you'll never forget.

Every event of crossing over is different. Some individuals have questions before they cross over, others have things they want to do first or they may want to be reassured that their family will be all right after they cross. You will find that every death and transition is not the same.

Communicate to the lost soul that they must look for the Light and begin to make their way towards it. It is important that before sending the lost soul into the Light, you call down any loved ones on the other side that would like to come and offer a hand for this soul who is making their transition. When the soul is greeted by familiar souls it will be comforted and the soul will now be more likely to make a smooth transition into the Light.

Testimony

Daddy's Little Girl

Joseph is truly a godsend! I found myself struggling to deal with the passing of my father, who was also my best friend. Our relationship was so close that no words could describe the bond we shared. I was truly 'Daddy's little girl'. On the day of my father's memorial, my aunt came across an ad on Facebook mentioning Joseph's show at *Renegades*, which really struck me in the heart, because out of all days to receive this information, why that day? Why would it show up when she's never been to *Renegades* or searched for psychic mediums? It compelled us to think that maybe it was a sign; after all. my dad was a Joseph too!

Instead of going to his show we decided to book a private session to guarantee that we would be read. Hopefully I would be able to reconnect with my dad and he could somehow bring me the closure I needed to piece together my broken life, as his passing had been so sudden and unexpected that it had left me devastated.

He was so young and had so much life ahead of him! I am in nursing school and have always had a passion to help and inspire others, but after my dad's passing it had been so hard to continue on. I would ask myself, "How am I supposed to lift others up when I can't even lift myself back up?" My biggest concern was if I had been there, was there anything I could have done to save him?

I was a little skeptical so I made the appointment on a friend's credit card and put the appointment under her name so I knew that he couldn't "research me" by Googling my name. I've never had a reading performed and I didn't want to make myself vulnerable to be more devastated after leaving his office, but it turned out to be the complete opposite experience. The second Joseph walked in he just had such a presence and light about him. He didn't ask any leading questions and he channeled my dad's spirit almost instantly. From the words he used, to his sense of humor, Joseph hit the nail right on the head.

He described my Dad's passing and reassured me that it was his time and that it happened so quickly that there was nothing in my power I could have done to change the outcome. Joseph reassured me that my dad is still with me in spirit every day of my life. He mentioned things that have happened after his passing and touched upon mostly everything that I had been beating myself up about or struggling to find answers to. Joseph then called me out on being skeptical and it was my dad who completely threw me under the bus by telling Joseph that I used a friend's name so he could not Google me. Gee, thanks, Dad! Joseph was a good sport about it and laughed it off.

Leaving his office I just felt such a sense of peace as though a huge weight had been lifted off my shoulders. If there was one skeptical bone left in my body, after my reading it was gone. He proved time and time again that my dad was there by mentioning things that were things he never could have known - even if he *had* researched me!

If anyone is struggling with the loss of a loved one, Joseph is your answer. He is such a loving and kind soul who truly touches your heart with his powerful messages and reassures you that there really is more to life and that your loved ones are always with you… just in a different way. Words cannot express how thankful I am to have had this reading with Joseph. All I can really say is that it was such a blessing and I can move forward with my life and with the peace and closure I so desperately needed.

Shawna F.

Signs Are Everywhere

Chapter Five

Life as a physical being does end, but our eternal soul lives on forever. That is why our loved ones who have crossed over reach out to us; they want to let us know that they are fine. When we receive signs from spirit, it is their way of sending us comfort and reassuring us that we are not alone. They may also reach out and attempt to connect with us in ways and at times that are different than we may expect. Often they will send us a sign to remind us of something significant at a critical time in our lives. Whatever or whenever they choose to do so, in my readings I find signs from loved ones can be very healing for my clients.

People often ask me how to recognize what kind of signs our loved ones send to us. I tell them that a sign from a loved one works as a trigger. It will be anything that triggers our memory of them such as a song, a scent, a feather or a penny. Signs are usually personally significant in some way, though often it is very subtle and can come in a number of ways that may be easy to overlook. Sending signs to us from their side to our physical plane takes a lot of energy and focus; a spirit must work hard to send them, though to us they may seem small and inconsequential.

Pay attention to every thing. Even the smallest thing can be a sign, especially if it is a little unusual or stands out in some way. Look also for meaningful occurrences that are personally significant to you, like hearing a husband's favorite song on the anniversary of his death or finding a forgotten letter from Mom on your birthday. If you feel like you've gotten a sign from your loved one, trust your gut feeling and take it as a validation that you are right. Trust that this is evidence that the soul of your loved one lives on. Here are a few common signs to look for after the passing of a loved one.

Dreams May Not Be Dreams

In the movie *Sixth Sense* there is a scene when Malcolm (Bruce Willis) appears to his wife Anna (Olivia Williams) in her dreams. This is when the body is in a REM sleep condition when most dreaming occurs. Since those in spirit are without a body and exist in an energetic form, they can and do communicate with you through the energy of your mind, thoughts, emotions, and imagination during your dream state. While you are dreaming, your mind is not filled with the everyday activity that normally utilizes your left brain. It uses more of your right brain, which is the side used for creativity, imagination, and intuition. Also during the dream state the ego is no longer busy blocking all subtle energy from the spirit world and keeping you focused on your physical reality.

Visitation dreams from your loved ones in heaven are much different than normal dreams. For starters, they are incredibly vivid and everything in the dream feels real. When you wake up from a true visitation dream you will feel certain that your loved one in heaven has contacted you. During the visitation they will likely send you messages as well as reassure you that they are in a good place.

There may not be actual words; communication is telepathic in the spirit world. They will show themselves as you remember them when they were in good health or as young and vibrant. They may even show you a glimpse of your future or some information that will help you or other living family members in your waking life

Electrical Energy

We are all energetic beings housed in a physical body. When we die we leave our physical body and become pure energy. Because they are now fully energetic spirits, our loved ones can interfere with the energy flow of electricity as a means getting our attention. There are a number of ways they can do this, such as causing the lights to flicker or by turning the TV, radio, or lights on or off. They can also cause things like appliances, phones, or children's battery-powered toys to turn on for no apparent reason.

I have heard stories from some of my clients telling me about how their cell phone rang with the deceased's phone number, only to be nothing but static when they answered the phone. Most of the time such electrical signs are just your loved ones wanting you to know they are with you. If your television turns on unexpectedly, pay attention to what show is on; there may be a message there. When you see the lights flicker on and off, remember what you were thinking about around that time, because it might just be confirmation on thoughts you were having.

Sensing a Presence

Believe it or not, your loved ones are often watching you from their spirit world. Now don't run to throw on a robe when getting out of the shower, because they don't see you in the physical form! They will perceive you as energy, color patterns, thoughts, and emotions, which is actually the exact same way that many people see the dead. It's all about energy. Feeling the presence of your crossed-over loved one is one of the top signs that they really are with you and visiting you from beyond the physical.

There are various ways that you may feel their presence. The most common is a shift of energy in the room that you may sense when your hair stands straight up on your arm or you get the feeling that you're being watched. During readings with clients, many of them have described feeling the presence of someone around them and experiencing tactile sensations such as having someone rub their back, touch their arm, or play with their hair.

The Power of Scent

I am known as a physical medium, which means that I'm able to tap into sensations of the deceased loved one and manifest them into physical forms like smells, raps, and knocks that members of the audience can perceive. These are also ways that our loved ones send us signs that they are present. If you are smelling certain scents such as cigar or pipe smoke, perfume, a specific flower, or even the aroma of foods like marinara sauce where there is no physical explanation, then you may be experiencing a sign from heaven from your loved one. They often reveal their presence by sending us scents that we associate specifically with them.

Scents are the strongest trigger in memory recall and they can really enhance our connection with our passed loved one. It takes a lot of energy for a spirit to manifest physical smells, so thank them for the gift by acknowledging that you know they are near.

Signs from Nature

Insects, birds, and animals are another favored sign that our loved ones use to let us know they are near and they are thinking of us. Because the spirit is pure energy they are able to channel their energy into God's creatures for a brief time to bring us a sign that their spirit lives on. When this happens the insect, bird, or animal will do something out of character that catches our attention.

I remember in one reading I kept seeing the image of a rooster flying around the house of the parents for whom I was reading as their son in spirit was laughing. The father confirmed that one day an actual rooster had flown into their garage and landed on his son's motorcycle and squawked at him. When he ran into the house to tell his wife, they came back out and saw that the rooster was now standing on the son's surfboard. It was obvious to me (because I could hear their son's amusement) that the rooster had indeed been a sign from him.

In other readings spirits will project to me an image of the family dog running excitedly around the home acting very happy to see them, while family members shake their heads and wonder why their dog is acting so crazy. Dogs and cats have far keener sensitivity to the astral realm; they can actually sense when a visiting spirit is present. If your dog is barking or wagging its tail while appearing to be staring at nothing that you can see, or your cat begins hissing or purring like someone is there, pay attention to these signs.

Movement of Physical Objects

At the beginning stages when the loved one is still in transition, he or she has the ability to move objects or place them in your path. Even when they move further beyond the physical, your loved one is able to move objects to get your attention. It can happen in several ways, like moving a framed picture or causing an object to fall. When this happens, say hello and know that your loved one is sending you a sign from spirit.

Objects can appear from nowhere as well. I had a group reading with two sisters whom had both lost their husbands. During the reading a penny dropped seemingly out of nowhere and rolled in front us. I thought it belonged to the women - and they thought it belong to me! We soon realized that it had not come from anyone physically present. Later they shared with me that they had made a necklace out of the ‘penny from heaven’.

Another sign I saw was a video of a grieving mother. Everyone is paying their respects at a funeral when suddenly a balloon drops out of nowhere from the ceiling and begins floating toward the mother. It floats down and across the room and stops in front of her face; she tries to bat it away but it comes right back and bumps into the back of her head. She pushes it away again only to find it returning and firmly pressing against her. That was a sign from heaven!

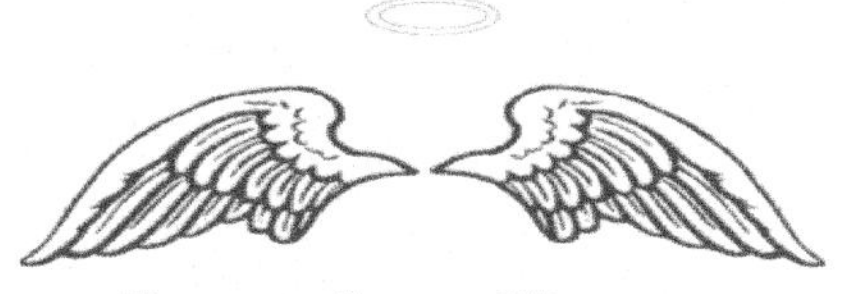

Penny from Heaven

Thank you, Joseph, for an incredible meeting. You are an amazing man to have your gift and to be able to comfort people that have so many unanswered questions. I have to say when I first sat down I was a little nervous, but you and your sweet disposition and soft voice put my mind at ease. It was so wonderful to be able to be close to my John through you. You touched on things that no one could possibly know. There were questions I needed answered and through you, John answered many. I know John is with me and as I told you today, I do feel him around me, and that does comfort me immensely.

Also being in the same room during that bizarre moment when that penny dropped from nowhere for Donna really blew my mind! Anyone that is a skeptic really needs to have a session with you. Again, thank you so much. It was more than a pleasure meeting you.

Alice D. - Palm City, FL

The Dead Speak to Us

Pay attention to thoughts that seem to pop into your head at just the right time, especially if it sounds like something your loved one would say. Often we dismiss many of the messages we receive from our loved ones as our own internal monologue. If you seem to be having thoughts of encouragement or answers to life questions that you are pondering, it most likely actually is the thoughts of your loved ones who are speaking to you. While your loved one can't audibly speak to you because they are not a physical being, they are able to communicate with you telepathically.

We simply must learn to trust that such communication actually came from them and that we are not making it up. One way to determine if it is your own thoughts or helpful advice from a crossed-over loved one is to listen to how the words are phrased. Look for phrases or word usage that are not a part of your normal vocabulary. Also, your loved ones will sometimes use other people to deliver their messages. Someone in your life might be a messenger unknowingly when they reach out to you with reassurance or guidance – or you may do the same for others!

I always tell my clients that heaven is within; that since our loved ones are energetic beings they will connect with us through our soul. Speak through your heart when you want to talk with your loved ones. Listen to your inner voice and begin to have a conversation within yourself. Let go of any expectation and pretend you are five years old again, freely using your imagination. Open up and let go; you will soon find that you are able to have a conversation with your loved one.

That is how I do mediumistic readings. I listen to the voice within and trust that it's your loved one. I state a few things that I am hearing from that voice and by your validation I confirm that I'm truly connected. It works better with mediums because we have no attachments or knowledge of the loved one so we can make uncensored statements. If you know the history of the loved one with whom you are connecting, it's sometimes hard for you to determine if you're making it up in your head. If you are properly tuned in to your senses, you will feel the basic truth of the information and you will be able to trust that you are truly communicating. As this happens more and more frequently your confidence in the process will grow.

Connecting Through Music

Have you ever had a certain song that keeps playing in your head that seems to have come out of nowhere? In my galleries it happens all of the time. I find myself singing lyrics of a song that connects the person whom I'm reading to their loved ones. (This can be quite comical at times since I can't sing!) Songs may also trigger memories of our loved ones, or we may find a message in the lyrics. Sometimes a certain song will play on the radio at the right time or repeatedly on many stations. I had a client tell me that the song 'Stairway to Heaven' kept playing on her iPod over and over until she turned it off.

Heavenly Timing

Have you ever had something happen that seemed to be just a coincidence, yet you somehow felt that it was not? Sometimes you might be looking for direction in life and suddenly someone gives you a flyer or business card directing you to just the right person, place, or event just as you need it. When something synchronistic happens in your life and you get the feeling your loved one in Heaven was somehow involved, you are probably right!

One woman I know had her vehicle totaled in a minor crash. It was a nuisance to find a new car and a challenge to find one at a price that the insurance payment would cover. One day her husband noticed a car on Craigslist being offered by a man named Harry. That had been her father's name and as soon as she heard about this car she just knew that her father was somehow helping her out from the other side. Sure enough, when they went to meet the seller, the car was perfect and a great price.

It was actually Harry's girlfriend who was selling a car that had belonged to her mother who had passed away a few years previously. She said something had told her to hold on and find the right buyer; it was odd but she almost felt like this was what her mother wanted. So this deal was brokered in heaven by not just one, but two kind and loving parents!

Seeing Spirits

I'm often asked why our loved ones don't show themselves. There are people who are strongly clairvoyant who can see spirits, but most people are unlikely to ever physically see deceased loved ones. People ask me if I can 'see dead people', as the little boy in the *Sixth Sense* movie famously phrased it. I don't see spirits anymore, but as a child I did. The last time was when I saw my grandmother when I was ten years of age as I described earlier in this book and the experience frightened me so much that I shut down that ability. Now I only see them in my mind's eye or as a shape that appears near a living person. I believe that the main reason more people don't see their dead loved ones as apparitions is because our loved ones intend to comfort us and let us know they're oaky, not to scare us with a ghostly appearance. You may see a vision through your mind's eye and feel it's your imagination, but when this happens try to focus on the details of their appearance and surroundings. There just may be a message there for you!

Seeing orbs is a very common form of visitation as well. They will often appear in photographs even when there was no visible sign of them to those who were actually present at the time the picture was taken. When people take photos of me during a live 'Speaking to Heaven' gallery, orbs will frequently show up all around me.

Butterfly Gift from Ron

I wanted to reach out to say that when Joseph did a reading for me, he mentioned that "butterflies" would be a sign from my husband. Well, I had an incredible experience recently. I was sitting by the lake near my house when a beautiful blue and brown butterfly landed on my leg, made its way to my palm and just stayed for the longest time turning slowly and stretching its wings as if to show me how beautiful he was. I say 'he' because I'm convinced this was Ron coming to me to say he was OK! It was truly the most beautiful butterfly I've ever seen - and it left me with a peace I haven't known since Ron died. Thank you, Joseph!

Blessings - Diane C.

Animal Heaven

Chapter Six

Over the years I have frequently been asked what happens when animals pass into the spirit world. People who have lost their beloved pets will ask me if animals continue to exist after they die and if they are able to communicate with us from the world of spirit as humans do. Almost everyone has lost a pet. They become part of the family and many couples that are childless treat their pets as if they were their own children. So what does happen to pets after they die? Do they even have a soul or go to heaven? Will we ever see our dearly departed pets again?

It is entirely possible to connect with animals in spirit. Many people who have had a near-death experience have said that pets were often among the first to greet them after they left their bodies. In my line of work as a medium I occasionally connect with pets in heaven, although it is not my strong suit. Mediums who specialize in communicating with animals are often referred to as pet psychics. Normally they are people with a very strong connection to animals. I call them the 'Doctor Doolittles' of mediumship.

What does the Bible say about what happens to animals after they die? Does a pet's emotions and ability to relate to human beings mean that animals possess an immortal spirit that will survive after death? Theologians say no. They point out that because man was created to be superior to animals, animals cannot be equal with men. Most interpretations of the Bible assume that man's likeness to God and animals' subservience to man implies that animals may have the "breath of life, but not an immortal soul in the same sense as man." (Genesis 1:26)

Then God said, "Let us make man in our image, in our likeness, and let them rule over the fish of the sea and the birds of the air, over the livestock, over all the earth, and over all the creatures that move along the ground."

However, animals are spirits just as plants are spirits; even the rocks and the minerals of the earth have some form of spirit life within them. I do feel that the souls of the animal kingdom are separated from the souls of humans for a reason, but it is not because they are inferior; it is because they on a different level. In my book ***"Is There More to Life Than What We Know?"*** my Spirit Guide Sparrowhawk explains the evolution of a soul. His interpretation will help to give clarity about whether or not an animal has a soul. The following channeled information is the story of a spirit's journey on Earth.

The First Level is Mineral An entity from another Universe is called a Star Child. If this entity requests to fulfill karma on the earth plane and has never lived on earth before, it must enter in the form of a level one soul; this level of energy manifests as mineral.The mineral soul is pure energy. Mother earth is billions of years old. She is alive. Her soil and minerals are filled with souls of pure energy.

The new souls to mother earth, the Star Children, have come from other galaxies and universes to the earth to learn. When they arrived, their souls became a part of Mother Earth by forming as a mineral. Like an earthworm that plows its way through the soil, this new energy will move through the earth.

The next time you pick up a rock or a crystal, pay attention to how it feels. You can sense that it is of pure energy. Have you ever talked to a mountain? They do have a soul. Consider enriching your spiritual journey by learning to talk with beings of this pure level of energy. They communicate with each other, why not with you? Those with the gift to see auras can see the energy of these mineral souls. They will glow and twinkle. They're in tune with Mother Earth's vibration. This is how the soul will learn about the earth; it's a part of her. When the soul evolves, it may stay as a level one or move to the next level.

The Second Level is Vegetation

Next the soul of pure energy, if it chooses, will manifest as plant life. It will pollinate a seed until the time is ready for it to surface and then there is a new world of being for the energy to express. Not quite letting go of Mother Earth with its roots planted firmly into her, the soul's new lesson is now about physical growth. Now the soul has entered into the earthly chain of evolution. The soul needs nourishment to survive; it's a physical form. It can reproduce by pollinating; the seeds are their young. The soul now will experience life and death.

The Third Level is Insects Those pesky little bugs actually have a soul! The third level for the soul is even more evolved physically. This is the first experience for the soul of having a body with organs. As an insect it will also become an aggressor as well as prey to other beings. It has the knowledge to organize and colonize. It has the ability to reproduce.

The Fourth Level is Animal

Mammals, reptiles, fish, and birds are all part of the animal kingdom. When the soul evolves to this level, it exhibits a strong instinct for survival. It becomes both the hunter and the hunted. At this level the soul as a being has emotions. There is an impulse to care for their young and for one another. This is the last level before a soul can choose to be human. Domesticated pets are generally the ones that will move on to the final level of being human.

The Fifth Level is Human

Humans are the caretakers of Mother Earth. They were sent here by God to take care of her. The animals were to be protected and the environment was to be kept clean. Love and friendship were to be shared among humans; this is how God intended the earth to be. This is the highest level of the soul in the three dimensional earth. By moving through other levels, humans have had the experience of Mother Earth. Human spirits cannot incarnate back to animal, plant or mineral forms, however.

Do Pets Reincarnate?

Pets do reincarnate within their soul groups consisting of the animal kingdom of insects, birds, fish, and wild animals as well as the domesticated kingdoms that include livestock and pets. As with humans, the group soul kingdom will reincarnate within their soul groups. The lion may come back as the elk or the rabbit becomes the wolf. In the domesticated animal kingdom farm animals will reincarnate as different livestock and the souls of pets return as future pets.

In the Bible it says that God gave us dominion over the earth, which actually means that our task is to take care of the earth and her inhabitants. It is our responsibility to help members of the 'lower' kingdoms move along in their spiritual progression. This is a big influence on the domestic animal kingdom because our pets become more 'human-like' in their interactions. These animals become even more intimate with humans and share in the 'human family' experience. They exhibit traits of loyalty and unconditional love and other characteristically human traits.

Animals Do Communicate Through Mediums

Losing a pet is so much more painful than many people realize. Often those who do not like animals or do not have a pet cannot understand how we can grieve so much for them. They do not realize that animals were very much a part of our family. As a medium, I do connect with the souls of animals but they sometimes appear to me as a surprise. They want their owners to know they are still with them and love them very much.

Animal spirits do not communicate in exactly the same way that human spirits do. They appear through clairvoyance just as human spirits do, but their communication tends to be simpler thought forms. Animals have not developed speech, yet they do communicate with us through telepathic thought forms and desires.

My dog Hoover was great at this. After the passing of my beagle Hoover, I would often catch glimpses of him in the corner of my eye when I would enter different rooms in the house. Some nights I could hear his nails on the tile walking around the hallway outside of my bedroom door; then I would hear him flop down with a sigh on the other side of the door. This went on for months until I moved from that house; then he stopped coming around.

Make sure to look for signs from your beloved pet after they pass. As with human spirits they may move small objects or you may think you feel a cold nose pressed into your leg. Some people have described seeing slightly indented spots on their furniture where a pet frequently sat when it was alive. Rather than feeling sorrow at these times, enjoy the moment that your pet has made the effort to create. Remember, your pet is no longer suffering and is totally free and at peace.

Pets do show evidence of their survival by showing themselves as they were while on earth or by conveying many of their character traits through symbols. I have often had a cat or dog in spirit jump on my lap during readings or private home parties. It must be quite strange watching me pet something on my lap when no one else can see the animal or hearing me talk to the animal out loud, saying things, like "Good boy!" I do get a few strange looks, but if I don't acknowledge the pets they will drive me crazy until I pay attention to them! In this they are very much like human spirits.

Pet Stories

One night during a public gallery I heard a name in my head that sounded Native American, 'Sunkmanitu Tanka Ob Waci'. When I tried to say the name out loud I screwed it up, but a woman at the gallery recognized what I was trying to say and corrected me. During the reading I had seen in my mind's eye a young running warrior with his hair blowing in the wind. He kept running and running and did not appear to be tired. I asked her who this guy was. She laughed and said, "That's not a guy - that is my horse! The name 'Sunkmanitu Tanka Ob Waci' means 'Wind in my Hair' and that was the name of my horse!"

During another reading I had with an elderly woman, I saw a young child on her knees praying. "She looks like an angel," I told her. "Also, she has a white fur stole around her neck. Who is she?" The woman laughed and told me, "That's my dog - Angel!"

Is There an Animal Heaven?

What I have experienced is that while animals will reincarnate right away we can still contact them or see them in heaven. Back to our movie, *"What Dreams May Come*"; there is a scene where Chris reunites with his Dalmatian in heaven. I explained in an earlier chapter how our thoughts become reality and we create our own heaven and in this heaven our pets can certainly be a part of it. Their soul is just as omnipresent as are the souls of humans and can be everywhere at once.

When animals are in spirit form they no longer need food for nourishment and the killer instincts are gone. As energetic beings they will reunite with their animal soul group and choose what species to reincarnate as in their next life. They may want to explore another kingdom as well and become more domesticated. The animal kingdoms are filled with millions of souls; there are plenty to go around for generations of lifetimes.

Prophets & Mediums

Chapter Seven

In both the Old and New Testaments of the Holy Scriptures we find that throughout history God brought forth prophets and mystics such as Abraham, Moses, Daniel, Jeremiah, and Elijah. These prophets were known as God channels and were at times honored by the church and at other times just as likely to be persecuted and face severe condemnation. Jesus laments that many people put prophets to death. Further evaluation among some modern bible scholars takes the view that the word 'prophets' as used here means 'messengers of God', or 'God's spokesmen'.

"O Jerusalem, Jerusalem, you who kill the prophets and stone those sent to you, how often I have longed to gather your children together, as a hen gathers her chicks under her wings, and you were not willing." Matthew 23:37

What served as law thousands of years ago as recorded in the bible has changed as Man has evolved in spiritual awareness. Throughout my life I have been subjected to judgment from some (certainly not all) Christians who preach that the work I do as a medium is demonic and goes against God's will and against the teachings of Jesus.

They claim that I'm not actually communicating with loved ones who have crossed over but rather I am being fooled by demons posing as the deceased, therefore I am working as one of Satan's minions. I decided to write this chapter to give my thoughts on the traditional view of prophecy and mediumship. Knowing as I do how the high vibrations of love and peace are always present when I connect souls across the dimensions of heaven and earth, it's sad and frustrating that this view should still be so predominant in this day and age.

Many in the world of metaphysics have noted me as being a modern-day prophet. Through my gift I hear God's message clearly, but if only the world could also hear what God is saying! He is always communicating with us. As we evolve, so does His message. The abilities to speak to the dead and foretell the future are spiritual gifts from God as well. They may occur in people who are not necessarily spiritual, but such individuals will not be able to fully access and develop their gift unless they have some type of spiritual program. That does not mean that they must adhere to any specific religion.

Many people confuse spirituality with religion. Religion has organized beliefs and practices, usually shared by a community who are guided by rules and rituals. Spirituality is more of an individual practice and has to do with having a sense of being one with God and the universe. It also relates to the process of developing beliefs around the meaning of life and the connection we have with others.

As discussed in an earlier chapter, a couple of examples of religious views that have been grafted onto the general psyche of humankind include the concepts of hell and the devil. When Jesus gave a description of hell he called it a destiny of sinners who refused to change their ways. He was speaking of the fate of souls who in earthly life were unable to realize their higher spiritual nature and achieve the life that God intended for man. In fact the quality of their lives would be the opposite of life in the way that God had intended. Such a fate could be likened to living in the torturous and fiery conditions of the local garbage dump outside of Jerusalem. This metaphor was unfortunately taken as literal historical information by church leaders in later ages.

Likewise the concept of the devil, or Satan, has been perpetuated throughout the ages to serve the purposes of men. In the Old Testament there is no mention of Satan. Satan is not an actual being but a metaphor for the power of temptation that is present in every human to do wrong. So it puzzles me as to why Christians preach that the work I do as a medium is demonic and satanic and that it goes against God and the teachings of Jesus, since Satan and hell do not actually exist! What *does* exist is negativity and hatred in the world and this is what I call hell today.

Christian views are divided when it comes to what happens after death. The Catholics believe in a heaven and hell. Other Christians believe that the deceased are in a sort of unconscious stasis until the second coming of Jesus. In stasis they are without a soul until Judgment Day, when those who swore allegiance to Jesus will be resurrected into physical bodies and live in a heaven on earth while those who did not swear allegiance to Jesus will be thrown into the fiery pit of hell.

These are the people who are the modern day 'witch-hunters' of mediums. They believe that since the soul is in stasis, it is not possible to communicate with the soul; hence mediums are being fooled by demons that trick people into believing that it's their deceased relative.

These teachings did not come from Jesus. Where is it written that when we pass over our soul goes into stasis until Christ returns? Jesus taught that the kingdom of God is here and that Heaven is within us, not in a far distant place. We are energetic beings of light housed in flesh. Heaven is connected to the Light and it is *actually through God that our loved ones communicate with us.* If everyone knew that we all have the power within us to talk to God and to our crossed-over loved ones, this would diminish the control of the church, so the church has demonized mediumship in order to hold the power and wealth.

There is evidence that Jesus knew there is an afterlife into which people go immediately after passing away. While on the cross Jesus spoke to the thief beside him, telling him that he would be with him that day in paradise. The most important lesson is that Jesus promised that his disciples and that all of us would be able to "do all the things he did and greater things". (John 1:50) Jesus was a person who did not judge or persecute people who did not see things the way that he did. No matter whether the person had a sinful past or lived like a saint, Jesus would embrace them as his brother or sister and remind us that in God's eyes everyone is created equal. I always ask myself, "What would Jesus do?" I believe that he would help those who seek him, heal the sick, and heal the pain of those who are suffering, such as those grieving for their passed-over loved ones.

Often when I'm being persecuted because of the work I do as a medium or healer, I hear the voice of Jesus in my head telling me that he, too, was persecuted and what really counts is how you serve God and not what others think of you.

I often do my research in the Old Testament because I know the Hebrew text has been transcribed word for word over the century without being altered. The New Testament, however, has been rewritten throughout centuries by kings and religious leaders to benefit the supremacy of whatever view their monarchy or clergy is attempting to spread, meaning that contents from the New Testament in the bible has been changed from its original content. If the Jews had believed that Jesus was the Messiah, his teachings would have been written in the Torah and preserved as original content unaltered by clergymen and kings.

The New Testament in its present form is not an exact record of the original content. For example, there are gospels of Mary that were banned from the bible. The text also reveals that Mary Magdalene may have been an apostle - perhaps even a leading apostle - not a prostitute. While some texts in the Bible seem to deny women a voice in the Christian community, the new findings help to spark the debate about the role of women in the church. It's difficult to imagine women having a voice in the dark ages. It was not permitted so the church banned Mary's gospels in order to keep women subservient. In time as scholars continue to analyze and interpret the original Hebrew writings, we will know more of the hidden truths of the original contents that were removed and changed in the modern day bible.

It is written in the Old Testament of how God warned the Israelites not to practice pagan ways. Spiritualists and mediums were common among the pagan peoples of the Bible lands. God warned the children of Israel against becoming involved in these practices just prior to their entry into the Promised Land of Canaan.

"When you enter the land the Lord your God is giving you, do not learn to imitate the detestable ways of the nations there. Let no one be found among you who sacrifices his son or daughter in the fire, who practices divination or sorcery, interprets omens, engages in witchcraft, or casts spells, or who is a medium or spiritist or who consults the dead. Anyone who does these things is detestable to the Lord." (Deuteronomy 18:9-12 NIV)

The last sentence - that *"anyone who is a medium or spiritist or who consults the dead"* being detestable to the Lord - well, naturally I have to disagree. As a prophet and a channel to the Ascended Masters I am connected to the God Consciousness and I am aware that these writings were written during a time of primitive thinking. We are no longer living in those times; the laws written then do not all pertain to our current time in history.

This was written in the Old Testament during a time when the high Priests of the Israelites feared that their tribes would be influenced by pagan ways, so they implemented the law that the penalty for anyone practicing spiritism was death. The fear of breaking God's laws was the only way to keep the Israelites from straying from their tribes; this is what made their nation strong. Consider the teaching of Moses; he was sent to free a nation from bondage. Jehovah channeled to Moses the Commandments for all the people of 'I Am' to follow. Moses had the people fear Jehovah in order for them to respect Jehovah; in that time and place fear was the only way to keep the people of 'I Am' obedient to Gods laws.

Jesus came along and changed everything. He brought forth the new teachings of Jehovah. He taught people that Jehovah was our Father and He had been sent by our Father to teach of love. Jesus was the true Son of God, the Son of the Father. The message that Jesus brought was that Our Father God comes in love. He taught that we should not fear God, but embrace Him, for He is love; all are created in our Father's image.

The human soul is as perfect as our Father God. We will dwell in our Father's Kingdom of souls and our eternal life shall never end. Jesus himself even contacted the dead when Peter, John, and James accompanied him to a mountain to pray. Two men appeared, 'in glorious splendor' and talked with Jesus. The three disciples recognized the two men as Moses and Elijah. So did the Son of God defy his father? The answer is no, here again is proof that contacting the afterlife is not a sin.

The human race must learn to grow and adapt to new teachings of God. We must believe there is something much greater than what we are experiencing now. Think of all of the spiritual knowledge that mankind has learned in the past and practiced through world religions such as Buddhism, Christianity, Islam and Judaism as a basic spiritual education for mankind. As we have evolved, our need for deeper instruction has evolved as well.

Take, for example, the 12 Universal Laws that discuss in detail the metaphysical underpinnings of our universe and help explain why things work the way they do in our world. Several of these offer us an idea of how we may further master our world. The 'Law of Oneness' explains that we are all in this together and that we live in a world where everything is connected. This is a simple concept to understand but not easy to either accept or live in accordance with.

At the same time, the 'Law of Perpetual Transmutation of Energy' tells us how we can actually make use of these laws to raise our energetic vibration and because higher vibrations consume and transform lower vibrations, we can make positive and lasting changes in our world. These are a few examples of a new level of spiritual wisdom that is infiltrating our worldview and allowing us to take what we have learned through ancient biblical texts and expand upon them with concepts that guide our efforts to master our world.

(For more information about the 12 Universal Laws refer to "The Light Shall Set You Free" by or simply Google "The 12 Universal Laws" and you will find a number of sites on the topic.)

The work of a medium today is to give closure and a sense of peace and to help ease the grieving process. Belief and acceptance in life everlasting is certainly not new, but what is new is the ability of the modern mind to understand the metaphysics of how mediumship works. Spiritualism is not to be feared; the beliefs center around the meaning of life and the connection we have with other souls. Today's mediums are here to be a loving bridge to the departed and to give witness that life goes on, even after death and that our loved ones are always and forever will be a part of our lives even after their death.

Speaking to Heaven

Chapter Eight

Celebrity mediums are paving the way for a skeptical public to be more open to those with psychic and mediumistic abilities. Through television and social media, mediums like John Edward, Lisa Williams, John Holland, and Theresa Caputo are creating awareness about intuitive ability and spirit communication. I remember when I first came into my abilities I was afraid to come out publicly due to the stigma and skepticism surrounding psychics and mediums, but I have noticed that as the media continues to showcase the work of mediums society has gotten a better understanding of the work.

The concept of a medium speaking to the departed does not seem so scary or feel as though it is against God's will. People are looking for closure; they love what they see on television and want the same experience for themselves. So it's important that we continue to have successful psychic mediums in the public eye that spread their message via television or by giving live demonstrations to educate society that mediumship is not a bad thing.

If you want to find a medium to speak with your crossed-over loved one, you may have a number of questions. Whom should you choose, a psychic or medium? What are the 'dos and don'ts' in hiring a medium? Are there different levels of gifted psychics and mediums and how do you choose the best? Are celebrity psychics or mediums better than others that are not so well known? Why do mediums charge different prices for their readings, and if it is a gift, shouldn't they be offering their services for free anyway? Are telephone readings and Skype readings as effective as face-to-face readings and is there a difference? How can you avoid the scam artist preying on the vulnerable; in other words, how can you be sure that the psychic or medium is legitimate? Can you contact your departed loved ones yourself? These are the types of questions I'm frequently asked by my clients about the work I do as a Psychic Medium and I will attempt to answer them in this final chapter.

When looking for someone who specializes in contacting the deceased, remember that not all psychics are mediums but all mediums are psychic. That is why I am known as a Psychic Medium; I do both psychic and mediumistic readings. If you are seeking information about your career, relationships, finances or anything regarding past, present, or future insights, a reading with a psychic is best. However, if you are seeking to communicate with a deceased loved one or one of your spirit guides, a reading with a medium is best.

Psychic readings given by a medium are different from traditional psychic readings by a psychic. Psychics do have second sight, or ESP (Extra Sensory Perception) which allows them to obtain certain information about a person without seeing it, hearing it, reading it, or using the other five senses. Some psychics use tools such as tarot cards, runes, playing cards or palmistry.

A psychic may also read a person's aura, the energy field that surrounds living things. They use their psychic gifts together with their interpretative skills and knowledge of divination. This gives them insight into the inquirer's past, present, and potential future. However, they are not usually able to tune into other spiritual entities such as crossed-over loved ones.

A medium that does psychic readings is in tune with their own spirit guides, who in turn help to offer guidance for others. The role of the medium's spirit guides is to help guide people to stay on track for their soul's purpose. That's why I compare myself to a 'Magic 8 Ball'; I tell people to ask me a specific question and my guides will come up with the solutions to their questions! When a medium contacts a crossed-over loved one, it is to receive messages from the afterlife. The objective of a medium's work is to prove survival of the human personality after death and to help the bereaved come to terms with their loss. A mediumistic reading is a direct intuitive link with the spirit world to give proof that we all survive physical death. It is best to look for a psychic medium when looking to make contact with the afterlife as well in finding direction in your life.

The worldwide web is a great tool for finding the right medium, so do the research! My clients were confident about hiring me because of the many positive testimonials about my work that are posted on my Facebook page and through psychic directory sites. Also, referrals from someone you know and trust are very helpful. Work from client referrals is how I keep so busy! If you're hesitant to trust testimonials from strangers, try asking for a recommendation from someone whose opinion you can trust. If a person you know had a great reading it is easy to trust that the medium is legit, but be aware that no two readings are the same and one person's experience can be different than that of another even from the same psychic medium.

You can learn a lot about a psychic medium just by visiting their website. I would hesitate to use a medium if they do not have a website or if their website looks too 'fly by night'. If they have put a lot of time, money and effort into creating a website, then they are more likely to be someone who takes their work seriously. It's also important that the website has a photo of the medium on the site. If they do not, I would wonder what they are hiding and if they are afraid of being recognized. Maybe the medium is not fully committed to their work. I believe a picture is worth a thousand words and we can learn a lot about a person by looking at their photograph.

I find that the more experienced the medium is, the more in tune they are to spirit. Lots of practice helps to increase the accuracy of a medium even if they may have a fair amount of raw talent. It's a good sign when a psychic medium gives demonstrations of his or her ability on stage in front of a live audience. It indicates a level of self-confidence in their own ability. I hold public and private galleries a few times a month. It's a lot more difficult to work with a crowd of people than it is to do a private setting. We are talking about the world of subtle energy here and things do not always go according to our schedule. It takes real skill and talent to bridge the two worlds in a public setting and the medium is vulnerable to skepticism, so if they are able to perform under these circumstances it shows that they are the 'real deal'.

Another way to know if the medium is legitimate is to look for articles that have been written about the medium by a newspaper or magazine. You will find that I list all of my interviews on my website. You will learn a great deal from the interviewer's perspective about the medium.

Some mediums will have their own radio show or attend as a guest on other shows featuring readings. I love doing free reading through the radio; it is a great way to showcase my abilities to the public. Also look for videos of the medium. Videos provide a good sense of the medium's personality and character, reading style, manner of speech and attention to detail. I'm always adding fresh new videos to my repertoire.

I find that as my popularity grows I have reading requests from all over the world to do phone or Skype readings, but some people wonder if they are just as good as an 'in person' reading. The best way I can explain how telephone and Skype readings work is to say that it's like being on a three-way phone call between you, your loved one and myself. The spirit of your loved one is omnipresent (which means being everywhere at once) so spirits can make contact and communicate anywhere at any time, for there is no time or space to restrict the process. All spirits communicate by telepathy. For me it's thoughts and feelings that allow me to receive the message. And yes, it does work just as well over the phone or through Skype as it does face-to-face.

Know also that it takes more energy for a medium to bring in loved ones when there is more than one person in the room. For the more deeply serious readings or for those who are recently bereaved it is recommended that the group be family related so the medium is reading the same family tree. If you decide to do a reading with friends, the medium will often get mixed messages because they are now dealing with more than one family tree. If the loved ones of your friend are more persistent then yours they will dominate the reading and your experience will not be as profound as theirs.

How often should one get a reading?

After having a session with a legitimate medium you will leave feeling good about having been reunited with your loved ones and very eager to do it all over again. However, my advice to my clients is not to be a 'medium junkie'. The reason your loved ones choose to come through is to let you know that they are fine and are still a part of your life. In the spirit world our loved ones have their own lives to live and would want you to move on with yours. Those who schedule a session with me too soon after the last session will most likely find that the information is about the same. I would wait at least one year for your next reading. That way your loved ones will be able to bring you new information relevant to your life concerning events that have happened since your last reading.

Life Decisions

Our loved ones often do assist us with love, support, insight and guidance. They do in fact help us in more ways then we even realize. Some clients expect their loved ones in Heaven to "fix" their lives, but we all have life lessons to learn and experience. No loved one can "fix" anything for you as much as maybe they would like to. Even if your loved one always tried to tell you what to do with your life (which in hindsight can be spiritually draining) they won't do so from the spirit world due to their knowledge of our right to free will. We are the only ones responsible for our lives. It's not a loved one's responsibility to tell us what to do or to do it for us. We have to make our own decisions and take responsibility for our choices and actions. Spirits of our loved ones cannot interfere with those lessons that are meant to assist us in our soul's growth.

How do mediums communicate with spirits who speak other languages?

Communications from spirits are thoughts and those thoughts are universal in language. Spirits that never spoke English are not speaking in words to the medium but they are transmitting thoughts and ideas telepathically so that the medium can easily understand them. The same goes for communication with infants and animals in spirit. Whether the communication is with a baby who never lived long enough to learn to speak or a pet that never spoke in human language at all, the spirit is transmitting telepathically.

Is it unethical to make money doing spiritual work?

I am often asked if my gifts are spiritual, then why do I charge for my services? There is a concept in the world that it is unethical to make money doing spiritual work. My answer is that we all have our gifts and talents and that while God certainly intended for us to share them with others, he also intended for us to have joyful and abundant lives. For example, I enjoy Christian Rock performed by musicians like Chris Tomlin and Mac Powell. These musicians are doing spiritual work and making a prosperous living. They are using their God-given gifts just as mediums do; yet nobody questions their motive. Many spiritual authors, personalities and even television show hosts are flourishing financially from the wonderful spiritual work they are doing in the world, so why should mediums be treated differently? There is nothing immoral or unethical about making money doing spiritual work.

Why do Mediums charge different Fees?

When inquiring about mediums you will find that prices for readings differ from one medium to the next, but it doesn't always mean that a more expensive medium is better. Celebrity psychic mediums are not necessarily better than unknown psychic mediums. Generally when the number of followers increases there is a greater demand for the medium's services so their fees will increase.

There may also be a difference between those who are working as mediums part time and full-time mediums. Mediums who work full time have to earn enough from their readings to pay all of their bills. We have to pay for rent or a mortgage, insurance, automobile expenses, food, clothing, utilities, and everything else, just like the rest of the world. There may also be office rent and utilities if the medium has a practice away from home. Returning emails and telephone calls takes a lot of time, so many mediums hire an assistant to help them get through it all which in turn costs money that must be earned back through readings.

I have researched price ranges for medium readings that vary from $100 to $400 per hour; some celebrity mediums charge as much as $800 an hour. On the average, full time mediums will do anywhere from ten to fifteen sessions a week working a fifteen to twenty hour week, so it is not like your normal '9-to-5' job. Mediums work fewer hours because it takes a lot of energy to give readings and we must balance and protect our life force energy. If we exhaust all of our energy serving the public, we risk getting seriously ill or having low life-force energy to function in everyday life. The fees for a psychic medium's services may appear to be on the high side, but only because people don't consider the big picture.

Validations

First of all, it's best to seek a reading when you are relaxed and undisturbed. Allow the medium to proceed in his or her own manner. During the reading, be aware that there is a need for you as the sitter to validate messages (confirm that you understand the message) as evidence that your loved ones are with you and wish to make contact. Once you have acknowledged any initial information by validating it, the messages will flow in more clearly. The more open and receptive you are, the clearer the messages will be. Don't be too quick to say no or resist information if it is not immediately familiar to you. When people do this it can distract the medium before the full message can be given. Also, if you wait to analyze things that were said during the reading until a later time, it will give you time to fully understand them.

The evidence that comes forth in the reading, whether big or small, is often part of a puzzle that spirit is giving to the medium. Sometimes the information cannot be validated at that very moment, but will come together later as the pieces of the 'puzzle' fall into place. Also, don't set yourself up for disappointment by expecting to hear a certain word or phrase in the reading because it may not come up.

Again let me stress how important it is to let the medium know when they are correct. Spirit manifests and provides evidence in many ways; cause of death, physical features, personality, names, number of children, memories, hobbies, symbols, and so on, so be open to validate whatever comes through from spirit.

You will receive the best readings if you come with an open mind and maintain a sensitivity to the world of subtle energy. If you come with the intention to 'test' the medium, then often the information will not be clear and you will have wasted your time and money. Also, like anyone else at work, the medium can have an off day. But the most important thing is you must be open and willing to believe that communication is possible and don't be too quick to resist information that you don't immediately understand.

Skepticism

Each psychic and medium is unique in their abilities and each and every session is different. Do not compare the abilities of one psychic or medium with another, because you will find everyone has their own technique. Keep an open mind and listen to the information coming through so that you can have a positive and rewarding reading.

By the same token, it is important to have a healthy skepticism about the medium and the process. Remember that no psychic can see the future with one hundred percent accuracy; if they say that they can, they are not telling you the truth. Also bear in mind that although there are some exceptions (e.g. a medium who is also an astrologer) a legitimate medium will generally not need to ask you for personal information such as birth dates, names, or photographs.

Warning About Scam Artists

People <u>do</u> need to be careful of greedy scam artists who are pretending to be legitimate psychics or mediums. I did an interview for ABC about the red flags to look for in order to avoid scamming psychics and mediums. These frauds are good at deceiving people, especially people who are grieving or going through a desperate time in life. Quoted here is the original story:

"Police dubbed their investigation 'Operation Crystal Ball' and arrested fraudulent psychics that performed tarot card readings, palm readings, astrology readings, numerology readings, and spiritual readings. The indictment alleges that the family 'told clients that they and their family members or friends would contract terrible diseases, suffer horrible financial hardships, and endure terrible catastrophes, and that loved ones who were already sick would not recover, and that their lives would remain haunted by evil spirits if they did not cleanse their money of those evil spirits.'

"Joseph LoBrutto III is a well-known psychic in Florida who has been featured in newspapers and profiled on television. LoBrutto said it can be easy to be taken advantage of by false psychics and that research or references from new age stores can be ways of avoiding scams. There are bad psychics and mediums out there as well, just like there are bad doctors. The psychic may be 100% accurate as a reader but still can be a scam artist. 'The big red flag is keeping you coming back. It should be just that one reading,' LoBrutto said. 'And if they say it's a curse or a hex, there's no such thing.'

" 'There is no spell. They are merely using fear to manipulate you. Never give money to any psychic or medium that promises to remove a curse or spell or purchase an expensive candle, crystal or any product that they say is going to remove a curse, a spell or bad luck. You are not cursed. Moreover, never give money to any psychic or medium that asks you to wire a large sum of money.' LoBrutto is appalled by the behavior of the group. 'It's a shame. It really ruins our reputation,' he said. 'Psychics are stereotyped as being con artists and this doesn't help at all!' "

Speaking to Heaven

Do you long to talk to a loved one who has passed away and wonder if you are able to do this yourself? The answer is yes, you absolutely *can* communicate with your loved ones! People have been talking with crossed-over loved ones since humans have been on the earth. It is not as hard as you think. Just talk to them! Talk out loud and speak to them in your mind; they can hear you. Think of the teachings of Jesus where he tells us that Heaven is within; well, here is where our loved ones are, right within our soul. We can hear them in our hearts.

Begin by simply quieting yourself and clearing your mind as though you were preparing to meditate. Sit in a location that is silent and free from distraction. Light some candles, play some music, and meditate first. This will increase your vibrational frequency and help you to make a solid connection. Now close your eyes and empty your mind of anxiety and thought. Focus on the memories of your crossed-over loved one when they were alive and healthy. See them as they appeared when living, not as you think they may now look in heaven. The more significant the image is to you, the easier it will be to establish a connection.

ability to talk with our crossed-over loved ones lies within anyone who can heighten his or her spiritual awareness, so be open-minded and trust that communication is possible. See yourself with them at the present and focus on your memory of them and on their face. At this time you will begin to feel their presence. Now you may want to ask them questions. Be aware that any answers you receive may come as thoughts, images or emotions. Use your mind when communicating with them; thought is the universal language.

Ask your crossed-over loved one a question after you have held that person's memory in your mind. Do not answer in the way you believe that person would answer. Instead, be patient until you receive a reply that you can be certain did not come from your own mind. I would begin with yes or no questions at first and then have a dialog with them. Pretend you are five years old again and using your imagination to have conversations with invisible playmates. Tell them how you love them and miss them and ask them if they can send you a sign to reassure you that they are still a part of your life. It is that simple! That is how I do it.

Thank you for joining me on our continuing journey of life and in particular through this book, our discussion of heaven. I hope that you have found something of interest and usefulness here that will allow you to believe what your soul has always been trying to tell you; that heaven is real and our loved ones are not dead. They have merely experienced that same powerful and beautiful transformation that we ourselves will some day undergo. Remember that heaven is only a breath away. Our earthly world is a mere echo of its beauty and grandeur, but as amazing as it may seem, heaven is our real home and our time here is like a trip or time away at school. In the grand scheme of 'forever', a mortal life is fleeting. But oh, what a wondrous thing it is!

Blessings - Joseph LoBrutto III

To see a world in a grain of sand
And heaven in a wild flower
Hold infinity in the palm or your hand
And eternity in an hour

- William Blake

THE PROMISE

The Metaphysical Teachings of Jesus

"The Promise" is a compelling account of the blessings that come through powerful spiritual insight and a firm belief in a higher power. The lessons taught by Jesus come alive with refreshingly new relevancy for modern times through Joseph's intriguing blend of New Age philosophy, Judaism, and Christianity.

In this telling of the story of Jesus, familiar events that were described in the bible are now told from the metaphysical perspective. Jesus attained the Christ consciousness and wants us to know that this consciousness is possible for all beings of this earth. If we believe in the Universal Life Force, we all can become One with the Universe and manifest greatness in our own lives.

As an Audiobook "The Promise" brings the story of Jesus to life with the narration of Joseph LoBrutto and the orchestrated music of renowned musician Man Parish.

Printed Book* Kindle * Audiobook

OurJourneyofLife.com

Universal Energy Cards

All beings in the universe communicate with one another by vibrations, sound and color. These cards were channeled by a person who claimed to be extraterrestrial and gifted to Joseph.. The color symbols on the cards are Universal Symbols that holds a certain vibration on each card that will serve a function. By placing your left hand over the cards you will notice heat resonating from some of the cards. Other cards will activate when you are in need of them. This means the card is activated and here is what to expect from each card.

OurJourneyofLife.com

Divine Affirmations Cards.

Each Divine Affirmation card represents a Master or Archangel who will invoke their Divine Energy into each Sacred Geometry symbol. Every card will have an affirmation starting with the words "I AM" meaning "God Within" that is invoked into every affirmation. Each Masters/Archangels will project a color to all seven Energy Centers (Chakras) in your body creating a healthy Mind, Body & Spirit.

OurJourneyofLife.com

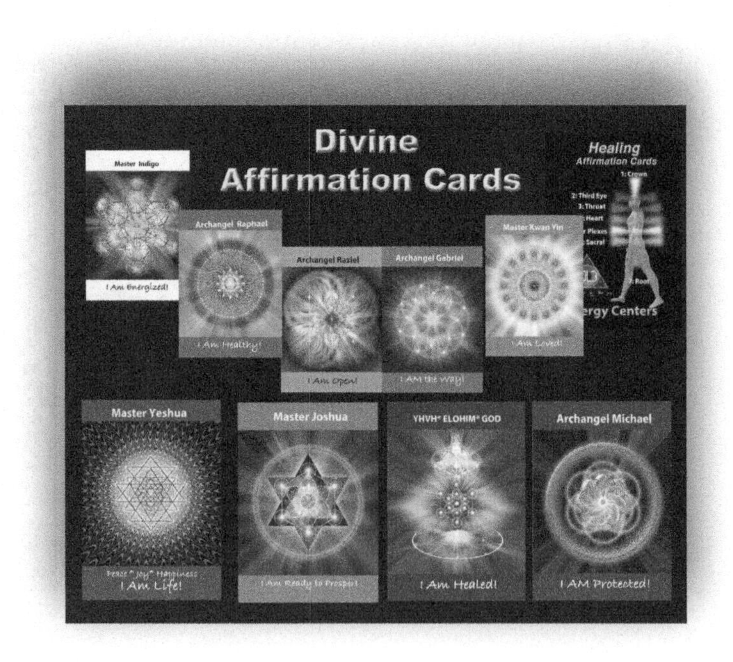

Divine Healing of the Mind * Body & Soul

Download Online or Purchase Download Cards

I AM- Healthy I AM- Healed** I AM- Loved****

This recording includes three meditations for the healing of the Mind * Body & Soul. During the healing process of this recording the Healing Masters/Angels will invoke the words 'I AM' as part of a Healing Affirmation along with a color during the healing. The word I AM means 'God within'. Using the words I AM will invoke the strength of God during the healing process. The affirmations and colors projected from the Healing Masters/Angels will be directed to all seven Energy Centers throughout the body creating a healthy Mind, Body, and Spirit.It was John of God who informed Joseph that he will be coming into his Divine Healing abilities. Today many have experienced miraculous healing of major diseases, physical, emotional trauma, depression along with receiving spiritual balance for a healthy Mind, Body & Soul.

OurJourneyoflife.com

Love * Forgiveness & Cutting Cord of Attachments

Forgive others as well as yourself in order to heal. The affirmations will help in cutting cords of attachments. Most importantly is to tap into the ultimate energy of Divine Love for attracting healthy relationships and true love.

Download Online or Purchase Download Cards

OurJourneyoflife.com

Protection * Fear * Phobias Emotional Trauma, Negitivity and Psychic Attacks.

We live in a world of beauty, harmony and perfection, but unfortunately humanity is playing its part in destroying that because we live a life that's based on fear, anger, hate and the wish to bring harm to other's. The divine energy and affirmations will be directed in helping you cope with your fears and phobias. Help you to heal from emotional trauma along with giving you protection from any negativity or psychic attacks.

Download Online or Purchase Download Cards

OurJourneyoflife.com

Our Journey Of Life

Our Never Ending Journey of Life Series

www.OurJourneyOfLife.com

Speaking to Heaven

Joseph LoBrutto III
Palm Beach, Florida

Corporate and Private Events

Joseph LoBrutto is available for events in your area, facilitating Messages from Spirit Galleries, Intuitive Workshops, Channeling Groups, Church or Spiritual Lectures, and Book Signings.

Joseph offers Private, Telephone And Group Readings

Made in the USA
Monee, IL
01 November 2021